WITHDRAWN

ethics, law and professional issues

a practice-based approach for health professionals

edited by

Ann Gallagher

and

Sue Hodge

palgrave
macmillan

First published 2012 by
PALGRAVE MACMILLAN

Palgrave Macmillan in the UK is an imprint of Macmillan Publishers Limited,
registered in England, company number 785998, of Houndmills, Basingstoke,
Hampshire RG21 6XS.

Palgrave Macmillan in the US is a division of St Martin's Press LLC,
175 Fifth Avenue, New York, NY 10010.

Palgrave Macmillan is the global academic imprint of the above companies
and has companies and representatives throughout the world.

Palgrave® and Macmillan® are registered trademarks in the United States,
the United Kingdom, Europe and other countries.

ISBN: 978–0–230–27944–0

This book is printed on paper suitable for recycling and made from fully
managed and sustained forest sources. Logging, pulping and manufacturing
processes are expected to conform to the environmental regulations of the
country of origin.

A catalogue record for this book is available from the British Library.

A catalog record for this book is available from the Library of Congress.

10   9   8   7   6   5   4   3   2   1
21 20 19 18 17 16 15 14 13 12

Printed and bound in Great Britain by
CPI Antony Rowe, Chippenham and Eastbourne

Contents

List of illustrations

List of cases

Airedale NHS Trust v Bland [1993] 1 All ER 821 (HL)
B (adult refusal of medical treatment sub nom Ms B v NHS Hospital Trust) [2002] EWHC 429
Barnett v Chelsea & Kensington Hospital Management Committee QBD [1968] 1 All ER 1068
Bolam v Friern Hospital Management Committee [1957] 2 All ER 118
Bolitho v City and Hackney Health Authority [1998] AC 232
Chester v Ashfar [2004] UKHL 41
Crawford v Board of Governors of Charing Cross Hospital (The Times, 8 December 1953)
Donoghue v Stevenson [1932] AC 562
Gillick v Wisbech Area Health Authority [1985] 3 WLR 830
J v C [1970] AC 688
McLoughlin v O'Brien [1983] 1 AC 410
Nettleship v Weston [1971] 2 QB 691
Pearce v United Bristol Healthcare NHS Trust (1998) 48 BMLR 118
Poland v Parr [1927] 1 KB 236
R v Arthur (The Times, 6 November 1981)
R v Bodkin Adams [1957] Crim LR 365
Re C (adult: refusal of treatment) [1994] 1 WLR 290 (FD); [1994] 1 All ER 819
R v Cambridge Health Authority ex p. B [1995] 2 All ER 129
Re Council of Civil Service Unions and Others (England) [1985] AC 374
Re E (a minor) (wardship: medical treatment) [1993] 1 FLR 386
Re L (medical treatment: Gillick competency) [1998] 2 FLR 810
Re MB [1997] Med LR 217
R v Secretary of State for Social Services and Others ex p. Hincks (1980) 1 BMLR 93
Re T [1992] 4 All ER 649
R ex p. Axon v Secretary of State for Health and Others [2006] EWHC 37 (Admin)

 Case from USA

European Court of Human Rights

List of statutes

Adults with Incapacity (Scotland) Act 2000
   s.1(2)
   s.1(6)
Children Act 1989
   s.1(1)
Data Protection Act 1998
Employment Rights Act 1996
   ss.43A–43K (inserted by the Public Interest Disclosure Act 1998)
Equality Act 2010
   s.6
   s.9
Family Law Reform Act 1969
   s.8(1)
Health and Safety at Work etc. Act 1972
   ss.2–8
Magna Carta 1215
Medicinal Products: Prescription by Nurses and Others Act 1992
Mental Capacity Act 2005
   s.1(2)
   s.1(3)
   s.1(5)
   s.2(1)
   s.3(1)
   s.3(2)
   s.4(6)
   s.4(7)
Mental Health Act 1983 as amended
   s.2
   s.3
Mental Health (Wales) Measure 2010
Public Health (Control of Disease) Act 1984
   s.2A (inserted by the Health & Social Care Act 2001 s.60)
Public Interest Disclosure Act 1998

Acknowledgements

The editors would like to thank all of the chapter authors, who gave so generously of their time and experience to make this book possible. This was very much a collaborative effort and an interesting and enjoyable journey for all of us.

We are grateful to colleagues in the School of Health and Social Care at the University of Surrey who, although not directly involved, supported the project. Other colleagues who advised us and assisted with practice examples include Malcolm Woollard, Neil Monery, Verity Snook, the Operating Department Practitioner teaching team and Denise Skidmore.

Ann Gallagher would like to thank Kiera for her forbearance during the writing process.

We are indebted to the team at Palgrave Macmillan, particularly Katie Rauwerda, for their encouragement, and the anonymous reviewers for their very helpful comments.

Notes on contributors

Kevin Acott

Kevin Acott is Mental Health Tutor and Branch Leader. He teaches across a wide range of undergraduate and postgraduate programmes the School of Health and Social Care at the University of Surrey. He previously worked as a practice development facilitator, a lecturer-practitioner and a community psychiatric nurse. Kevin adapted S. Videbeck's *Mental Health Nursing* for a UK readership.

Helen Allan

Helen Allan is a nurse and registered nurse teacher. She works at the School of Health and Social Care at the University of Surrey. Her areas of interest are the management of emotions in nursing and health services, fertility and reproduction, nursing role development and the impact of these areas on caring and qualitative research methodologies. She has published extensively on mentoring, supervision, sociocultural aspects of reproductive health and professional education.

Anne Arber

Anne Arber has a clinical background in cancer nursing. She is with the School of Health and Social Care at the University of Surrey. Her research programme involves the examination of interpersonal processes in team meetings, information-sharing strategies in supportive care following a diagnosis of lung cancer and support for informal carers. She has expertise in discourse analysis and mixed-methods research.

Anna Brown

Anna Brown has been involved in midwifery education for the past 11 years in both pre- and post-registration midwifery programmes at the University of Surrey. She has developed research interests in education and, at the time of writing, was working on teaching and assessment of midwifery students "being with women" after winning the Dame Rosalind Paget Award and the Iolanthe Trust Award for 2010.

Pat Colliety

Pat's professional background is child health and health visiting and she now teaches on the child health and public health programmes. She has also been involved in European projects promoting approaches to deal with cyberbullying and has co-authored a training manual and book on the subject. She also teaches ethics to undergraduate and post-graduate nursing students at the School of Health and Social Care at the University of Surrey and has led a project which uses theatre studies students to work with nursing students to explore ethical scenarios through the medium of improvised acting.

Ann Gallagher

Ann Gallagher is Reader in Nursing Ethics, Director of the Inter national Centre for Nursing Ethics at the University of Surrey and editor of the journal *Nursing Ethics*. She has published widely on healthcare ethics and is co-author of *Ethics in Professional Life: Virtues for Health and Social Care* (with Sarah Banks) and *Nursing and Human Rights* (with Jean McHale). Ann has extensive experience of teaching ethics and of research and clinical ethics committee activities.

Sue Hodge

Sue Hodge was admitted as a solicitor in November 1969. She works in the School of Health and Social Care at the University of Surrey. She left private practice to teach more than 20 years ago. She contributes to the development and delivery of undergraduate and post-graduate programmes for healthcare professionals with reference to law and ethics. She has been Principal Examiner for the Law of Torts for the OCR Examination Board Advanced level GCE in Law. She has published widely on health care law, including *Tort Law* and *Unlocking Torts* with Chris Turner (3rd edition, 2010).

Khim Horton

Khim Horton is Senior Lecturer (Clinical) Care of Older People in the School of Health and Social Care at the University of Surrey. She is a registered nurse and nurse teacher with a clinical background in medical and gerontological nursing. Her research focuses on aspects of ageing studies, telecare, nursing and nurse education, using both qualitative and quantitative research methodologies.

Jane Leng
Jane Leng qualified as a nurse and worked as a staff nurse and ward manager on a neurosurgical unit. She was employed as a nurse tutor at Cuckfield and Crawley School of Nursing before moving to the University of Surrey. She has been a fellow of the university Centre for Excellence in Teaching and Learning and has developed innovations in relation to digital storytelling for ethics education.

Deborah Macartney
Deborah Macartney has clinical experience as a nurse practitioner and is now Senior Tutor and Director of Studies in the School of Health and Social Care at the University of Surrey. Her role is to support the educational development of health and social care practitioners. Deborah has worked with the National Patient Safety Agency on educational materials and currently delivers clinical risk management education to develop student understanding of patient safety in the healthcare system.

Nuri Pansari
Nuri Pansari has a background in mental health nursing. She developed an interest and expertise in ethics while working at the University of Winchester before moving to the School of Health and Social Care at the University of Surrey. Nuri was Head of Programme from 2005 to 2010. She is now retired and enjoys travelling.

Sue Ryle
Sue Ryle has extensive experience of nursing practice and education. She has worked in surgical areas, was a ward sister in a urology department and has extensive experience of teaching and programme management. Sue is Division Lead for Quality Assurance at the University of Surrey.

Steve Searby
Steve Searby has experience in adult nursing in pre-hospital and hospital care. He served with HM Forces before joining the School of Health and Social Care at the University of Surrey in 2009. He

teaches on the foundation degree and undergraduate professional programmes.

Caroline Wade

Caroline Wade at the time of writing worked in the School of Health and Social Care at the University of Surrey. She is a critical care nurse with commercial sales education and higher education experience. She is committed to creating innovative educational strategies to enhance the professional development of evidence-based acute and emergency care practitioners, whose practice is underpinned by a broad range and high standard of legal and ethical principles.

Chapter 1

Introduction

Ann Gallagher and Sue Hodge

As a health professional or student of the health professions you are required to develop a wide range of new knowledge, skills and professional values. An understanding of ethical, legal and professional issues is essential to help you to: maintain professional standards, to negotiate dilemmas in your everyday practice and to respond effectively should you witness unprofessional practice. You may already have some experience of health services as a patient or relative or you may have gained experience as a practitioner. In any case, it is likely that you may feel uncertain regarding the right responses in situations such as the following:

- You are working in the operating theatre and it becomes clear that the anaesthetised patient who is to have a surgical procedure requires a circumcision to gain access to his bladder. He has not given consent for this. The patient's wife directs the surgeon to proceed with the circumcision. The surgeon asks for your opinion. What would you say and why?
- You are a member of a paramedic crew and you arrive at the home of an elderly couple. You are confronted with a chaotic scene. The woman has a bleeding arm and her husband, who has dementia, is lying on the floor with a head injury. The woman refuses to let you take her husband to hospital. What would you do and why?
- You are working on the Accident and Emergency Department when a 14 year old is admitted with severe abdominal pain. A routine pregnancy test is positive. The teenager insists that you do not tell her parents. What would you do and why?

▶ You witness a colleague being disrespectful towards a couple who have learning disabilities. The woman is pregnant with their first baby. What would you do and why?

The ability to give an account or to explain the reasons for your actions and omissions is an essential component of your professional accountability (see Chapter 2). The clinical reasons for doing one thing rather than another should be based on evidence or research. As a health professional you must, however, also consider the well-being and preferences of patients and family members in the context of care. At times, as in the examples above, there may be a conflict between what you think is in the best interests of patients and what they or a relative wishes. The ability to provide sound ethical, legal and professional reasons for your actions and omissions is essential. As you work through this book you will have the opportunity to explore these, and other, examples of scenarios and to develop an understanding of appropriate responses and the reasons you can give to underpin them.

In this introductory chapter we introduce you to key ethical, legal and professional concepts that are examined in this text, that is, accountability, consent, truth telling, confidentiality and justice. First, we will say something about the nature of ethics, law and professional issues in healthcare.

What Is Healthcare Ethics?

Ethics is an unavoidable part of healthcare practice. It is concerned with reflection on values, with making decisions, with doing the right thing and, it can be argued, with the development of good character. It is important to be able to distinguish between factual and ethical issues in healthcare. Questions such as 'how many people are on the waiting list for a hip replacement?' and 'which treatment saves most lives following a myocardial infarction?' are factual or evidence-based questions. Questions such as 'how should we allocate scarce healthcare resources?' and 'in what circumstances should we withhold treatment following a myocardial infarction?' are ethical or value-based questions.

There are different branches of ethics and two are particularly relevant to this text: normative ethics and descriptive (non-normative) ethics. Normative ethics, concerned with what people *should* or *ought to* do or how they *should* live, is most closely associated with moral philosophy. Examples of questions associated with normative ethics include: Should the patient be told the truth about her diagnosis? Should the confidentiality of a teenager be maintained when she refuses to tell her parents that she is pregnant? Descriptive ethics is concerned with what people do, think and believe in relation to ethical issues in healthcare practice. This branch of ethics straddles moral philosophy and, most commonly, the social sciences. Empirical ethics questions include: What are nurses' views of assisted suicide? What are patients' perspectives on dignity in relation to their care? How does ethics teaching contribute to the development of ethical sensitivity? Whereas normative ethics involves thinking or ethical analysis and the application of rules, principles and theories to practice situations (the focus of this text), empirical ethics generally involves data collection from questionnaires, interview, focus groups or observation. The data are then analysed, findings reported and recommendations made.

Healthcare ethics, then, refers to a wide range of practice situations. There are few decisions, actions or omissions that do not have an ethical dimension. Engaging with the scenarios, activities and discussion in each of the chapters enables you to reflect on your own practice and to rehearse how you will respond to ethical issues in the future. It also has the potential to make you more competent and confident in dealing with ethical complexity and uncertainty in everyday practice. There is a rich literature in normative and descriptive ethics to draw on that will illuminate your practice. Overall, healthcare ethics is concerned with doing the right thing and with being a certain kind of person in healthcare situations. Ethical analysis and empirical ethics research findings help with this. In addition to reading texts such as this one, we recommend that you read articles on topics of interest in journals such as *Nursing Ethics*, *Journal of Medical Ethics*, *Bioethics* and *Ethics and Social Welfare*. Texts that will provide you with an overview of issues and approaches relating to healthcare ethics include those by Davis et al. (2006), Fulford et al. (2002) and, more broadly, Steinbock (2007). The *Encyclopaedia of Applied Ethics*, the *Encyclopaedia of Bioethics* available in some university libraries and the online *Encyclopaedia of Philosophy* are also useful resources (http://plato.stanford.edu/).

Approaches to Healthcare Ethics

You have been introduced to two branches of ethics (normative and descriptive ethics). This section focuses on normative ethics, on the principles and theories that help people think about and justify decisions, actions and omissions in everyday healthcare practice. There are many possible theories and principles that you might appeal to and it is not possible to do justice to all of them here. However, it is helpful to know something of the range of options and how to learn more. Box 1.1 summarises the main types of ethical theory.

Box 1.1   **Ethical theories**

Duty-based theories – This focuses on the duties or obligations of healthcare professionals. It is an approach that underpins many professional codes. In moral philosophy this is referred to as deontology and the philosopher most associated with this theory is Immanuel Kant (Kant 1785, Paton 1948, Baron et al. 1997). There are some very helpful prescriptions within deontology. One of the best known is 'you must not treat others merely as a means to your own end', that is, you must respect individuals for their own sake and not merely as resources to help you achieve your own ends or goals. A key question to ask from a duty-based perspective is: what are my duties or obligations as a healthcare professional?

Rights-based theory – A right is defined as a claim you can make that is justified on the basis of international or national rights frameworks. Some rights are described as 'positive' in that they require something of others and some rights are 'negative' in that they require that people are left alone with no interference. Reproductive rights can, for example, be of both kinds. A positive right to reproduce suggests that if a couple is infertile they should be offered fertility treatment. A negative right to reproduce suggests that couples should be allowed to reproduce without interference. Negative rights might be appealed to if, for example, a couple had severe learning disabilities. It is likely there would be debate as to whether they have or have

→

not a right to reproduce. It is argued that there is a 'correlativity' between rights and duties or obligations because duties are necessary to make rights meaningful (Beauchamp & Childress 2009). If, for example, no individual or government has a duty to provide healthcare then it is unhelpful to talk of a right to healthcare. Rights-based approaches to healthcare ethics are particularly strong in emphasising the global context and transcultural nature of ethics (Macklin 1999; Klug 2000; McHale & Gallagher 2003; Hunt 2007). Key questions to ask in relation to rights are: what are patients' or service users' rights? What are my rights as a healthcare professional?

Consequence-based theory – One of the most common consequence-based ethical theories is utilitarianism. The two philosophers who developed this approach initially are Jeremy Bentham and John Stuart Mill (Mill 1789). Contemporary utilitarians include John Harris (1985) and Peter Singer (2001). The slogan the 'greatest happiness for the greatest number' relates to utilitarianism. In a healthcare context utilitarians focus on the question: what will lead to the most benefit and least harm for most people? This approach is particularly helpful in relation to resource allocation in healthcare but less helpful at the bedside.

Virtue-based theory – The previous three theoretical approaches can be said to focus on the actions or conduct of the healthcare professional, that is, doing my duty, respecting rights and weighing consequences. A theoretical approach that focuses on the character and ethical qualities or dispositions of the healthcare professional is virtue ethics. There is a growing literature relating to virtues and healthcare (see, for example, Crisp 1996; Swanton 2003; Banks & Gallagher 2009) and discussion continues as to which are the most relevant virtues for healthcare professionals. In the discussion in the chapters you will, for example, come across references to professional wisdom, respectfulness, honesty, integrity, courage, compassion and justice. A key question relating to a virtue-based approach to healthcare ethics is: what virtues (dispositions to think, feel and act) do I need to demonstrate in my everyday practice?

The theoretical approaches outlined in Box 1.1 do not exhaust the possibilities for ethical theory. There is, for example, a growing body of work on relational ethics, ethics of responsibility, hermeneutic ethics and ethics of care. Developments in ethics of care are particularly interesting for health professionals. Special issues of the journal *Nursing Ethics* (Issue 2, 2011) and of the *Journal of Ethics and Social Welfare* (Issue 2, 2010) have explored the potential of ethics of care for health and social care practice. Given the many options regarding ethical theory the reader may feel rather overwhelmed if not confused. All of these theories throw light on the moral life and help us to think through the ethical implications of decisions, dispositions and actions. They may also conflict and point to different ways of thinking and deciding.

It is our view that ethical approaches should be: easy to grasp; provide a helpful framework for thinking; and be applicable to everyday practice issues. One ethical perspective that continues to be written about and applied to practice is the 'four principles approach'. This has been written about by healthcare ethicists such as Beauchamp and Childress (2009), Gillon (1985) and Edwards (2009). This approach has also been criticised for being overly simplistic and too mechanistic. It is a helpful framework but needs to be approached critically and thoughtfully. It is, therefore, only as good as the way it is used. Box 1.2 outlines the approach.

Box 1.2   **Four principle approach (4PA)**

Respect for autonomy – The word 'autonomy' comes from two Greek words *autos* and *nomos* meaning self-rule or self-government (Beauchamp & Childress 2009). There are different theories of autonomy, some requiring a high level of cognitive functioning. The Beauchamp and Childress approach focuses on 'normal choosers who act, intentionally with understanding and without controlling influences that determine their action' (ibid: 110). They allow that actions can be autonomous 'by degrees' and that for an action to be autonomous it requires 'only a substantial degree of understanding and freedom from constraint' (ibid: 101). The principle of respect for autonomy acknowledges the individual's 'right to hold views, to make choices, and to take actions based on their personal values and beliefs' (ibid: 103). It

→

supports rules or obligations to: tell the truth, respect privacy, maintain confidentiality, obtain consent and help others to make decisions (ibid: 104).

The principle of non-maleficence – This requires that healthcare professionals should not inflict harm on others. It has a long tradition in healthcare and is often considered in relation to beneficence, as principles to do good and to avoid harm go hand in hand. The rule 'one ought not to inflict evil or harm' relates specifically to the principle of non-maleficence (Beauchamp & Childress 2009: 151).

The principle of beneficence has a long tradition in healthcare and, as has been said, is generally considered in relation to non-maleficence. In medicine, for example, the Hippocratic oath refers to both principles: 'I will use treatment to help the sick according to my ability and judgement, but I will never use it to injure or wrong them' (ibid: 149). The principle of beneficence supports rules such as: 'one ought to prevent evil or harm; one ought to remove evil or harm; one ought to do or promote good' (ibid: 151). Reflecting on the principles of non-maleficence and beneficence, therefore, requires a weighing up of what it means to do good as opposed to what will bring about harm or wrong. The principles are similar to consequence-based theories but need to be considered in relation to both the principles of autonomy and justice.

The principle of justice is one of the most challenging principles to grasp and apply to everyday practice. The concept 'justice' refers to 'fairness, desert (what is deserved) and entitlement' (Beauchamp & Childress 2009: 241). In healthcare ethics, justice is generally applied when there are challenges regarding resource allocation. Distributive justice, therefore, refers to a range of principles that suggest what fair or justice distribution is, for example, allocation on the basis of need, effort, contribution, merit or give everyone an equal share (ibid: 243). When resources are scarce, difficult decisions have to be made as to how to allocate resources fairly ensuring that the criteria are ethical and people are not discriminated against without good reason. Beauchamp and Childress (2009:241) put it this way: 'Standards of justice are

$\rightarrow$

needed whenever persons are due benefits or burdens because of their particular properties or circumstances, such as being productive or having been harmed by another person's acts. A holder of a valid claim based in justice has a right, and therefore is due something. An injustice involves a wrongful act or omission that denies people resources or protections to which they have a right.' Justice has also been discussed as a key virtue for health and social care professionals (Banks & Gallagher 2009).

The four principles approach has limitations but is also very helpful in structuring our thinking as we analyse and discuss ethical problems and make decisions that underpin our actions. The key questions in the ethical analysis of a healthcare issue would include:

- Is this patient/service user autonomous?
- What does it mean to respect their autonomy in this situation? For example, tell the truth, provide information, maintain confidentiality or respect privacy?
- What are the benefits to be gained from the interventions/omissions proposed?
- What are the harms or wrongs that might follow from the interventions/omissions proposed?
- What is the most just response in this situation?

A supplementary question but, we think, a necessary one would be:

- What virtues or ethical dispositions are required to do the right thing in this situation?

What Is Healthcare Law?

The law is a means of regulating society. It can be used to oppress people, for example, in any totalitarian state, or it can be used to protect people's rights and freedoms and to support a particular way of life. Each country in the United Kingdom has its own law and legal system meeting the country's own needs. The basic principles in each country are similar although details may be very different. In this book, we are primarily concerned with the law as it applies in England. We have made specific reference to the law as it is elsewhere where it is important to do so. You should be aware, however, that differences may well become more widespread and important as devolution takes its course. In relation to the provision of healthcare services, England, Scotland, Wales and Northern Ireland have their own different systems subject to the overall duty to provide healthcare services.

Why Is Law Important in the Delivery of Health and Social Care?

The law is used to:

- regulate professional qualifications;
- ensure competent practice;
- protect the rights of patients/clients;
- give someone harmed a right to be compensated;
- support ethical principles of special relevance to healthcare.

It is essential that all health and social care professionals have at least a basic understanding of the law as practice must always be within the framework provided by the law. Failure to follow the rules can lead to liability to pay compensation, dismissal from employment and loss of the right to practice, which are a few potential consequences of practice which does not reach an acceptable standard.

Where Do We Find the Law?

Life would be so much easier for everyone if there were a simple set of rules telling us what ought to be done in any particular situation. Unfortunately no such set of rules exists and we are left to make our own decisions in accordance with the law and are accountable if our decision or our practice is not lawful.

The law most relevant to readers of this book is found in:

- **Common Law** – principles developed by the courts over the centuries since 1066; for example, the tort of trespass to the person which gives us a right to compensation if we are touched without having given consent;
- **Legislation** – also known as Acts of Parliament or statutes – which must be obeyed and can generally only be changed by Parliament;

- **Treaties of the European Union** – principles which underpin all EU law, for example, protection from discrimination on the grounds of gender, disability, sexual orientation, race;
- **The European Convention of Human Rights** – among other issues the Convention forbids torture, inhuman or degrading treatment (Art 3) and protects our right to privacy and family life (Art 8).

Where to Find Explanations of How It All Works?

Case law

Law reports contain brief summaries of the facts relevant to the particular case, an explanation of the relevant part of the law and how it works and a decision in the particular case. Reports are available going back to the 11th century. The importance of a case depends on the status of the court in which it was decided. The most important courts in England are the Court of Appeal and the Supreme Court (formerly the Judicial Committee of the House of Lords). Once a case has been decided, any future case on similar facts involving the same point of law must be decided using the principles of law as explained in the earlier case – the doctrine of precedent. In some limited circumstances the Supreme Court (formerly the Judicial Committee of the House of Lords) may reach a different decision, changing the precedent.

Cases decided in other courts, for example the European Court of Justice and the European Court of Human Rights, are also very important and will influence the way in which English cases are decided. European law can in some circumstances overrule national law or lead to a change of law.

Textbooks and journals

Books are an attempt by the author to explain the law in an accessible way. Journals are a useful means of keeping up-to-date with changes.

Statutory Codes of Practice

Acts of Parliament can be very long and detailed and almost incomprehensible to anyone who is not used to reading them. To help understanding and thus to ensure good practice, Parliament authorises the creation of statutory codes, for example, the *Mental Capacity Act 2005*

Code of Practice. These Codes must be followed in all cases unless good reason can be demonstrated in a particular situation for taking some other course of action.

Professional Codes of Practice, Guidance

While not the law, Codes of Practice/Guidance are carefully drafted by the relevant professional organisation to ensure that in the vast majority of cases, following the rules will not only meet the appropriate professional standard but also ensure that the practice is lawful. As you read through this book you will find many references to the Codes published by the Health Professions Council (*HPC 2008*) and by the Nursing and Midwifery Council (NMC 2008, reprinted with numbered paragraphs 2010). At the time of writing, May 2011, the Health Professions Council has agreed a new set of generic standards which will be implemented on a rolling basis over the next two years as the Health Professions Council (HPC) reviews the standards of each of the professions. (HPC *New generic Standards of Proficiency accessed at www.hpc-uk.org*)

An Outline of Some Laws of Special Relevance to Health Professionals

Are Employees Protected by Their Employers?

An old idea was that employers had control over the way in which employees carried out their duties, including the right to specify what should be done and how. This gave rise to the doctrine of vicarious liability whereby an employer is liable for the wrongdoing of employees in the course of their employment. Cases which illustrate the difficulties of deciding whether an act is within the course of employment include the following:

Poland v Parr [1927] 1 KB 236

An employee assaulted a boy to stop the boy from stealing from the employer's wagon. The boy fell under the wagon and his legs were injured. It was held that the employer was liable although the assault on the boy had not been expressly authorised. The employee was acting reasonably to protect the employer's property which by implication he was authorised to do.

Rose v Plenty [1976] 1 WLR 141

Milkmen were forbidden to use a child helper on their rounds delivering milk. A milkman continued to use a child helper who was injured due to the milkman's negligence. The employer was held to be liable because the employee had been carrying out his duties although in an unauthorised manner. His actions had been in the course of his employment and for the employer's benefit.

A health professional is therefore protected to the extent that the employer will be liable for any wrongful act committed in the course of employment. This can include liability for negligence, trespass on the person and breach of confidentiality. Generally the employer will not be able to reclaim any compensation paid from the employee.

Negligence

The tort of negligence is used to ensure that where poor, incompetent or inappropriate practice causes a person harm or injury, that person is able to obtain compensation. It is difficult to define 'negligence'. The lay person might say that it means carelessness; a lawyer might talk about duty, breach and damage. Cases over the years have attempted to provide an explanation by using principles which help to decide what duty is owed and to whom and to set a standard of reasonable behaviour. Past cases are useful examples of how the rules work but every case will be decided by applying the relevant principles to its own particular facts.

In order to succeed in a claim for compensation, the victim of alleged negligence must generally prove that:

- the perpetrator owed the victim a legal duty of care;
- the perpetrator was in breach of that duty;
- as a result of that breach, the victim suffered injury or loss.

A legal duty of care is owed to any person whom we ought reasonably to foresee might be affected by our act or omission. In essence this requires us to carry out a 'risk assessment' before undertaking any activity. If any risk of harm is identified, we must put reasonable precautions and safeguards into place to minimise the risk. An early case about negligence which illustrates each of these points is:

Donoghue v Stevenson [1932] AC 562

Mrs Donoghue went into a cafe with a friend who bought Mrs D a bottle of ginger beer. Mrs D drank half the bottle but when the rest was poured into her glass, out floated the remains of a decomposing snail. Mrs D was made ill both by the nauseating sight and the impurities which she had consumed. The judges decided that the manufacturer of goods which reach the consumer untouched by anyone else owes a duty of care to that consumer. The manufacturers had clearly failed to take reasonable steps to ensure the purity of their product and, as a consequence of that failure, Mrs D had suffered damage of the type or kind which was reasonably foreseeable. She was awarded damages.

There will only be legal liability for negligence if harm has been caused by our act or omission. Where no damage or harm has occurred, the professional may still face disciplinary action by employers and/or the professional body governing practice.

The effect of these rules in the context of healthcare is that any person undertaking a task is under a duty to carry it out competently. Professionals must refuse to undertake a task where they lack competence. This may not be easy (or popular with colleagues and/or employer) but the courts make no allowance for lack of experience and/or training. The courts will judge competence on the basis of the way in which a competent professional would have carried out the task in the particular circumstances relating to the particular patient. A fairly modern case which illustrates these points is:

Wilsher v Essex AHA [1987] QB 730

Baby W was born 3 months prematurely. He suffered retrolental fibroplasias which caused his sight to be severely impaired. It was argued that the injury was caused by the negligence of a junior doctor who had failed to notice that a catheter used to measure oxygen had been put in a vein rather than an artery meaning that Baby W had been given too much oxygen. While the judges had sympathy for the junior member of staff involved, they emphasised that patients are entitled to expect that treatment is delivered by someone competent to give it. In the Court of Appeal, it was stated:

> The law requires the trainee or learner to be judged by the same standard as his more experienced colleagues. If it did not, inexperience would frequently be urged as a defence to an action for professional negligence. (per Glidewell LJ)   →

An additional problem faced by Baby W was that the causal link between the oxygen problems and the impairment of his sight could not be established – the damage was possibly caused by other problems suffered by Baby W. In the event, the claim was eventually settled out of court.

The duty of a professional is to act with the level of competence that is required by the circumstances. The decision will be based on the principle known as the Bolam principle:

> A doctor is not guilty of negligence if he has acted in accordance with a practice accepted as proper by a responsible body of medical men skilled in that particular art. (*Bolam v Friern HMC [1957] 2 All ER 118, 121*)

While this may suggest that all the professional needs to establish is that other professionals would agree with the action, a later case established:

> the court has to be satisfied that the exponents of the body of opinion relied on can demonstrate that such opinion has a logical basis. ... [and] the experts have [considered]...comparative risks and benefits and have reached a defensible conclusion on the matter. (per Lord Browne-Wilkinson in *Bolitho v City and Hackney Health Authority [1998] AC 232, 242*)

In simple terms, this appears to mean that judges, while having little or no medical knowledge, must nonetheless be satisfied that the opinion can be justified on an appropriate basis. Alternatively, the judges will require to be satisfied that the opinion is 'evidence based'.

Consent

Both civil law, through the tort of trespass to the person, and criminal law, the crimes of assault through to murder, reinforce a person's right to exercise choice in relation to personal and bodily integrity and to have that choice respected (the right to autonomy). As you are unlikely to intend to harm your patient and therefore unlikely to be faced with allegations of criminal behaviour, this part of the book concentrates on the civil law.

Trespass to the person can take three forms:

- **Assault** – putting a person in fear that they may be touched;
- **Battery** – touching a person either manually or using some type of instrument;
- **False imprisonment** – preventing a person from exercising freedom of movement.

When any aspect of trespass happens, compensation is payable regardless of the fact that no harm has actually occurred. The fact of consent, either by the person concerned or by virtue of law, is a complete defence to any legal claim alleging trespass.

It may seem that provided the patient agrees, the health professional will be protected but this is not always so. A patient may say that consent would not have been given had they properly understood the implications of the treatment or the attendant risks. Such a person has no claim using trespass but may succeed with a claim in negligence based on failure to give sufficient information. It might appear that in order to protect the health professional, a patient should be informed *in full detail* of all the facts, especially those relating to potential side-effects and/or risks no matter how small. This may be the case in other jurisdictions but in England the patient needs to be told about all relevant facts so that an informed decision can be made. What this means precisely is the matter of debate. This issue is discussed in detail in Chapter 3. Generally the Bolam principle will apply so that the health professional must ensure that the patient is given the information which a responsible body of professional opinion believes to be necessary in the particular circumstances (*Sidaway v Bethlem RHG [1985] 1 All ER 634*). In the more recent case of *Chester v Afshar* Lord Steyn reiterated the surgeon's duty to warn the patient in general terms of possible serious risks. He went on to explain:

> In modern law medical paternalism no longer rules and a patient has a prima facia right to be informed by a surgeon of a small but well established risk of serious injury as a result of surgery. (*Chester v Afshar [2004] UKHL 41,* para. 16)

You may quite reasonably believe that the legal rules are less than clear – how in fact should the health professional approach the issue of giving information? Help is available in guidance published by the Department of Health (*Good Practice in Consent DoH (2nd ed 2009 Introduction at para.1)*) which states:

> Patients have a fundamental legal and ethical right to determine what happens to their own bodies. Valid consent to treatment is therefore absolutely central in all forms of healthcare, from providing personal care to undertaking major surgery.

Both the Nursing and Midwifery Council (NMC), Code (2008, paras. 13–17) and the HPC Standards (2008, para. 9) emphasise the duty of the health professional to ensure that consent is given, the patient having been fully informed and involved in making the decision to consent to or refuse treatment.

The issue of consent is further complicated in the case of two groups of people namely:

▶ Adults who lack capacity;
▶ Children.

The rules are discussed in detail in Chapter 4. The following paragraphs provide a summary of the law.

In the case of adults the position is governed by the *Mental Capacity Act 2005* (*MCA 2005*). It must be remembered, and is stated by the Act in s.1(2) that 'A person must be assumed to have capacity unless it is established that he lacks capacity.' In other words, the person alleging incapacity must establish the facts on which this assumption can be justified.

Once it is established that a person is unable to make a personal decision, that is the patient cannot understand the information relevant to the decision, cannot retain that information, cannot use or weigh the information in the process of decision making or cannot communicate any decision (*MCA 2005* s.3(1)) then the health professional must make the decision in the best interests of the patient (*MCA 2005* s.1(5)). In determining a person's best interests, the health professional must take into account the patient's wishes and feelings (*MCA 2005* s.4(6)) as well as the views of others' involved with the patient, where it is practicable and appropriate to consult them' (*MCA 2005* s.4(7)).

The rules governing decision making on behalf of children are found in the *Children Act 1989* (*CA 1989*). In any decision relating to a child under the age of 16 years, the child's welfare is the 'paramount consideration' (*CA 1989* s.1(1)). The effect of this requirement is to make the interests of the child the sole consideration. This has been explained by Lord McDermott:

[This amounts] to a process whereby , when all the relevant facts, relationships, claims and wishes of parents, risks, choices and other circumstances are taken into account and weighed, the course to be followed will be that which is most in the interests of the child. (*J v C [1970] AC 688*, pp. 710–711)

Although the case was decided before the *Children Act 1989* was passed, the explanation remains useful to establish what the 'welfare principle' actually requires.

Confidentiality

It may be taken for granted by most people that all personal information about health matters will be treated as confidential by those to whom disclosure is made. It is clearly important that this belief proves well founded if the necessary trust between the patient and the health professional is to be maintained.

Information does sometimes have to be disclosed. The NMC makes it clear that a patient should be informed how and why information may be shared with others providing care (NMC Code (2008, paras. 5–7). The HPC tells health professionals that information must be treated as confidential and used only for the purpose for which it has been provided (HPC Standards 2008, para. 2).

Information may always be disclosed with the consent of the patient and to others who need to know in order to provide appropriate care for the patient. This extends not only to other health professionals but also to relatives who are providing care. Disclosure may also be made to a third party if the public interest or the patient's welfare requires it, for example, in matters raising child protection issues which must always be brought to the attention of those responsible for protecting the welfare of children, usually the Local Authority.

Additional protection of confidentiality is found in Article 8 of the *European Convention on Human Rights* which protects an individual's right to respect for privacy and family life. In deciding whether Article 8 has been infringed the circumstances in which the information is given to the patient are important – would the patient assume that confidentiality applies, would disclosure be to the patient's detriment?

The legal remedies available for breach of confidentiality are limited to:

- an injunction to prevent publication (in reality of limited effectiveness as it requires the person to have forewarning that disclosure will be made);
- damages which are generally available only where there has been financial loss.

In real life, the common law is not much help but statutes can be more effective. The *Data Protection Act 1998* gives people the right to access information about themselves, including access to medical records. There is a right to correct any stored information which is wrong. The person may also require the cessation of the processing of the data if continuing to do so would cause substantial distress.

In the context of the delivery of healthcare, greater protection is provided by the professional bodies which may take action for breach of the professional codes. Disclosure is now governed by guidance setting out what, how and why may be disclosed. The NMC published *Raising and escalating concerns – Guidance for nurses and midwives* in 2010. The HPC published *Raising and escalating concerns in the workplace* also in 2010. At the time of writing, the Guidance has only been very recently published. How effective it will be has yet to be seen but a valuable tool seems to have been created.

The problems raised by confidentiality are discussed in more detail in Chapter 6.

A Way to Protect Yourself from Allegations of Incompetence, Unprofessional Practice or other Breach of the Codes

'Records';
'Records';
'And yet more records!!'

The need for accurate records relating to the delivery of care cannot be over-emphasised. Record keeping is an important component in the process of caring for the patient as the record will often provide the only contemporaneous account of what happened. The NMC Code requires 'clear and accurate records' to be kept (paras. 42–47) while the HPC states 'You must keep accurate records' (para. 10). What makes a good record? Whatever form the record or part of it takes, handwritten, e-mail, correspondence or any other form, it should be factual and accurate. The recorded facts are the basis of any judgment made by the health professional. Remember that the legal standard of care is determined by the Bolam principle. Having the facts on which the judgment was based available means that the competence of any treatment or other decision can be assessed more effectively. Was the decision within the range of decisions which would be made by a competent practitioner in the specific circumstances of the case in question?

The NMC states:

> Records should ... be legible ... [and] not include unnecessary abbreviations, jargon, meaningless phrases or irrelevant speculation. Guidance (2009, reprinted with numbered paragraphs 2010) paras. 1–16)

While the Guidance is specific to NMC registrants, the principles are appropriate for all record keeping. Observing the principles is an effective way to create good records.

What Professional Issues and Guidelines Are Relevant to You as a Healthcare Practitioner?

Being a professional or being a student of the health professions requires more than rote learning or repetition of a series of activities. Being a professional means that you can 'profess' something, that you have some ideas or aspiration to do good and to make things better for individuals, groups and society. This requires a good deal of knowledge of, for example, physiology, pharmacology and psychosocial aspects of care; a wide range of skills, for example, in communication, teamworking, leadership and negotiation; and an understanding of the value base or ethics of your profession. Codes of professional practice or ethics specify what is required of your particular profession. This relates closely to professional ethics described as 'the agreed standards and behaviours expected of members of a given professional group and as described in that group's code of professional conduct' (Fry & Johnstone 2008: 16). The Nursing and Midwifery Council (NMC) and the Health Professions Council (HPC) codes and other relevant documents provide guidance regarding what is expected of a healthcare professional. It is important to be aware of the contents of your professional code and also to consider how your code differs from the codes of other professionals.

It is recommended that, in addition to becoming familiar with the contents of your own professional code, you examine the codes of your colleagues. You can locate their codes by accessing the websites of their professional bodies, for example, the Health Professions

Council, the Nursing and Midwifery Council or the General Medical Council (GMC). This activity will provide you with some insight into the range of professional issues you need to understand. You will also now be aware of concepts and issues common to all of the health professionals' codes (for example, consent, best interests, confidentiality and accountability) and to the different ways professional obligations are set out.

Introducing Professional Codes of Practice and Guidance

While not the law, codes of practice/guidance are carefully drafted by the relevant professional organisation to ensure that in the vast majority of cases, following the rules will not only meet the appropriate professional standard but also ensure that practice is lawful. The codes/guidance are also useful in spelling out what is reasonably to be expected from the professional.

Professional codes have a number of important functions. These include:

- **External function** – Codes confirm and support professional identity – how do we want to be? They can also reassure the public.
- **Internal function** – Codes are a guide, giving confidence and promoting reflection on the nature of professional practice.
- **Defining (professional) responsibilities in a relational context** – Codes provide guidance on negotiating relationships and boundaries with patients, service users, families and other professionals.
- **Disciplinary use of an ethical code** – Codes also guide disciplinary panels as they make decisions about poor and unethical practice. They specify professional expectations of individual professionals (Verpeet et al. 2005).
- **Political function** – Codes also have a political function as they point to what the profession stands for and the standards of that profession. A code may also be used to argue for more resources should these be inadequate (Chadwick and Tadd 1992).

You may already have begun to consider the overlap among ethical, legal and professional issues. All three areas are necessary for professional practice. Figure 1.1 illustrates this:

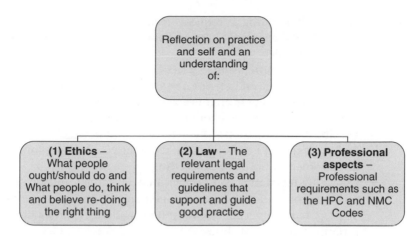

Figure 1.1 Doing the right thing in healthcare practice

 Why Study Ethical, Legal and Professional Aspects of Healthcare Practice?

In addition to the requirements of your regulatory bodies (Health Professions Council and Nursing and Midwifery Council), there are a wide range of reasons why and understanding of these areas is helpful and necessary:

- ▶ **Research and technological developments** – new drugs and healthcare interventions are constantly being introduced in healthcare and we need to ask 'just because we can do it, should we?'
- ▶ **Resources** – there is potentially infinite demand and finite resources in healthcare and decisions have to be made regarding how to allocate resources fairly. In addition to higher level funding decisions you also have to make and justify decisions regarding how you allocate your time in practice.
- ▶ **Changing expectations of patients** – patients now have much higher expectations and are increasingly aware of their healthcare rights and privileges as set out, for example, in the NHS Constitution (2010). Professionals have to be able to understand their responsibilities as they respond to these expectations.
- ▶ **Information accessibility** – the internet has opened up many new opportunities for learning about health status and treatment

options. Responding to requests from patients requires an understanding of the evidence base and of the values underpinning professional practice.

▶ **Reports of unprofessional practice** – there have, unfortunately, been many media and research reports detailing poor practice. It is hoped that learning from this text will equip you to maintain good practice and reduce the likelihood of poor practice.

▶ **Possibility of litigation** – if you have a good grasp of ethical, legal and professional issues it is unlikely that you will fall foul of the law or other disciplinary proceedings.

▶ **Changing legislative and policy contexts** – policy and legal developments continue to be implemented and discussed. You need to be prepared to enter the debate and to challenge policies that compromise professional ethics.

▶ **Professional status and registration of healthcare professionals** – accountability is an important part of being a professional. Knowledge of ethical, legal and professional issues will enable you to give an account of your practice, providing arguments to support one course of action rather than another.

There are, therefore, many good reasons why you should engage with these aspects of professional learning. We hope you will find learning from this text engaging and interesting with direct relevance to your everyday healthcare practice. We encourage you to discuss the scenarios and content with other professionals, students and also with friends outside healthcare, sharing perspectives and gaining new insights.

Overview of Chapters

In each of the chapters that follow you will be introduced to two scenarios focusing on particular professions and patient/service user groups in relation to key ethical, legal and professional concepts. The discussion in each chapter makes reference to the implications for different patient groups. The scenarios invite you to engage with real practice situations that have been anonymised and it is recommended that you consider how you would respond and why before you read the authors' discussion. An important reason to engage with the content of this text relates to your professional accountability, where you give reasons for your actions and omissions. This is the topic of Chapter 2. Chapters 3 and 4 deal with consent – when patients have capacity and when capacity may be compromised. Later chapters explore issues of truth telling (Chapter 5), confidentiality (Chapter 6) and justice (Chapter 7). Chapters 8 and 9 enable you to engage with the meaning of professional and unprofessional practice. Although the scenarios in each chapter focus on two of five professions (that is, nursing, midwifery, paramedical practice, occupational therapy and operating department practice), the content is relevant to all health professionals.

Conclusion

This chapter has introduced you to ethical, legal and professional aspects of your everyday practice. The overview should help you to begin to see how each of these three aspects of practice inter-relate and how an understanding of this can enhance your practice. We hope you enjoy your journey through the text and that you will engage with other practitioners and students as you think about and develop a critical understanding of these fundamental concepts in relation to your practice.

References

Banks, S. & Gallagher, A. (2009) *Ethics in Professional Life: Virtues for Health and Social Care*. Palgrave Macmillan, Basingstoke.

Baron, M.W., Petit P. & Slote, M. (1997) *Three Methods of Ethics*. Blackwell, Oxford.

Beauchamp, T.L. & Childress, J.F. (2009) *Principles of Biomedical Ethics*. 6th Edition, Oxford University Press, Oxford.

Bolam v Friern HMC [1957] 2 All ER 118, 121.

Bolitho v City and Hackney Health Authority [1998] AC 232, 242.

Chadwick R. & Tadd W. (1992) *Nursing Ethics: A Case Study Approach*. Palgrave Macmillan, Basingstoke.

Chester v Afshar [2004] UKHL 41, para. 16.

Council of Europe (1950) *European Convention on Human Rights*.

Crisp, R. (Ed.) (1996) *How Should One Live? Essays on the Virtues*. Clarendon Press, Oxford.

Davis, A.J., Tschudin, V. & de Raeve, L. (2006) *Essentials of Teaching and Learning in Nursing Ethics: Perspectives and Methods.* Churchill Livingstone/Elsevier, Edinburgh.

Dept. of Health (2001) *Good Practice in Consent.*

Donoghue v Stevenson [1932] AC 562.

Edwards, S. (2009) *Nursing Ethics: A Principle-Based Approach* 2nd Edition, Palgrave Macmillan, Basingstoke.

Fry, S.T. & Johnstone, M-J. (2008) *Ethics in Nursing Practice: A Guide to Ethical Decision Making.* 3rd Edition, Blackwell Publishing, Oxford.

Fulford, K.W.M., Dickenson, D.L. & Murray, T.H. (2002) *Healthcare Ethics and Human Values.* Blackwell Publishers, Malden.

Gillon, R. (1985) *Philosophical Medical Ethics.* Wiley, Chichester.

Harris, J. (1985) *The Value of Life: An Introduction to Medical Ethics.* Routledge, London.

Health Professions Council (2008) *Standards of conduct, performance and ethics.* HPC, London.

Health Professions Council (2010) *Raising and Escalating Concerns in the Workplace.* HPC, London.

Health Professions Council *New Generic Standards of Proficiency.* www.hpc-uk.org/mediaand events/news/index.asp?id=374, accessed 9 May 2011.

Hunt, L. (2007) *Inventing Human Rights: A History.* W.W. Norton & Company, New York.

J v C [1970] AC 688, pp. 710–711.

Kant, I. (1785, 1959 Edition) *Foundations of the Metaphysics of Morals.* Bobbs-Merrill Educational Publishing, Indianapolis.

Klug, F. (2000) *Values for a Godless Age: The Story of the United Kingdom's New Bill of Rights.* Penguin Books, London.

Macklin, R. (1999) *Against Relativism: Cultural Diversity and the Search for Universals in Medicine.* Oxford University Press, New York.

McHale, J. & Gallagher, A. (2003) *Nursing and Human Rights.* Butterworth Heinemann, Edinburgh.

Mental Capacity Act 2005 TSO.

Mill, J.S. (1789, 1962 edition) *Utilitarianism.* Fontana Press, London.

Nursing and Midwifery Council (2008 reprinted with numbered paragraphs 2010) *The Code: Standards of Conduct , Performance and Ethics for Nurses and Midwives*. NMC, London.

Nursing and Midwifery Council (2010) *Raising and Escalating concerns – Guidance for Nurses and Midwives*. NMC, London.

Nursing and Midwifery Council (2009 reprinted with numbered paragraphs 2010) *Record Keeping – Guidance for Nurses and Midwives*. NMC, London.

Paton, H.J. (1948) *The Moral Law*. Hutchinson, London.

Sidaway v Bethlem RHG [1985] 1 All ER 634.

Singer, P. (2001) *Writings on an Ethical Life*. Fourth Estate, London.

Steinbock, B. (Ed.) (2007) *The Oxford Handbook of Bioethics*. Oxford University Press, Oxford.

Swanton, S. (2003) *Virtue Ethics: a Pluralistic View*. Oxford University Press, Oxford.

Verpeet, E., Dierckx de Casterle, B. Van der Arend, A. & Gastmans, C. (2005) Nurses' views on ethical codes: a focus group study. *Journal of Advanced Nursing*, 51(2), 105–195.

Wilsher v Essex AHA [1987] QB 730.

Chapter 2
Accountability

Sue Ryle

Health professionals have to account for their actions by referring to the law – including their employment contract – to ethics and professional guidelines. As a professional, you are answerable for your actions and must be able to define, explain and evaluate the results of your decisions in relation to each of these areas. It will also be important to be able to refer to the evidence or research base that underpins your actions and omissions.

Accountability applies to everyone involved in the provision of health care. As a health professional it is important that you are clear about the meaning and implications of accountability both for you and for the organisation in which you practice. At the most basic level, accountability involves you being able to explain the reasons for your actions and omissions in your everyday practice. It involves your ability to explain why you opted for one course of action rather than another and, crucially, *why* you acted or omitted to act in that way. You need to be able to refer to the evidence or research that underpins your actions and omissions and also to the ethical, professional and legal arguments that support your practice activities. Accountability provides a very important rationale for you to work towards understanding and engaging with the content of this text applying learning to your own practice. When asked questions such as: 'why did you respond to the patient in that way?'; 'why did you opt for that course of treatment or care?'; 'why did decide to respect, or not respect, the wishes of the patient or the family? You need to be able to give an account and to refer to the ethical, professional and legal reasons.

This chapter enables you to consider accountability in the context of your professional practice as a nurse, midwife, paramedic, operating department professional or other health professional. The chapter also examines different kinds of accountability – professional, ethical, and legal – and discusses the different reasons that justify actions and omissions. These reasons or explanations are derived from the evidence and research base of practice and also from the value base of professional practice. Evidence-based practice and values-based practice are both necessary for professional accountability; however, this chapter focuses on the value and legal basis of practice.

Two scenarios will be presented that reflect situations through which the issue of accountability can be explored. They will be returned to later in the chapter.

As you read the scenarios please have two questions in mind, if you were the professional:

▶ What would you do?
▶ Why would you respond this way?

Scenarios

A paramedic's predicament

You are a paramedic responding to a 999 call. A young woman has fallen from a horse in a very remote part of the countryside. On examination you suspect a mid-shaft fractured femur but there may also be a neck injury. A four by four vehicle has been requested but this has been delayed and may take up to 45 minutes. The patient is in severe pain despite your having administered the maximum dose of 20 mg of morphine. The woman's systolic blood pressure (SBP) is 110 mmHg after the morphine has been administered. On a pain numerical rating scale score (NRS) she rated her pain as 7 post-morphine.

Pressure to prescribe

You are a nurse with experience of working in an acute cancer centre for the last four years. Your role is Chemotherapy Sister and you work in a nurse-led chemotherapy clinic. You have recently successfully completed the non-medical prescribing course to enable you to prescribe medication and to manage toxicities (chemotherapy side-effects) in patients receiving chemotherapy. It is a busy day and one of the nurses from the chemotherapy suite comes into the nurse-led clinic to ask if you would prescribe an alternative anti-emetic for a patient, Mrs Banks, who forgot to tell the doctor she saw earlier that day that her current anti-emetic was not preventing sickness. The doctor has now left the hospital for an outside clinic.

You are running late with the clinic and feeling under pressure to see the patients who are waiting. You also need to get all the chemotherapy prescriptions into pharmacy before the deadline at 1pm. You are persuaded by the nurse to write a prescription for Metoclopramide 20 mg intravenously to have with her chemotherapy that day. The nurse is really grateful and hurries back to the chemotherapy suite. An hour later, the emergency buzzer sounds in the chemotherapy suite and, as required, you respond and go to help manage the situation. You arrive to find that Mrs Banks is having trouble breathing, is feeling sweaty and is developing a rash. She appears to be having an anaphylactic reaction and when you look at her notes, you see that on the original history sheet, it states an allergy to 'Maxalon' (which is the recognised trade name for Metoclopramide).

Accountability: Background and Definition

Accountability is not a new concept. As the roles of health care professionals have gradually expanded, professionals have become more autonomous and taken on more responsibilities. This has resulted in an increased burden of professional accountability. Evidence-based practice and the requirement for a rationale behind decisions are crucial in the provision of safe care and to maintain public confidence.

It is important to highlight the fact that in parallel with this emphasis on professional accountability there has been a change in the way that the general public views the provision of health care. People are generally far more knowledgeable about the service and the care that they are given having easy access to an increasing number of information sources. In addition, society is increasingly litigious, with individuals seeking to gain compensation for any problems associated with the care that they are given. There is a growing emphasis on patient information and patients' rights, putting pressure on professionals and the organisations in which they work.

Hood and Pepper (2006) emphasise that accountability is being responsible and answerable for behaviour and outcomes that fall into the remit of a professional role. They state that 'professional nurses practice accountability each time they answer questions for reasons behind actions, document interventions and outcomes of delivered care and participate in clinical competency programmes' (Hood & Pepper 2006: 321). Accountability is fundamental to all health care professions and every professional must consider this in all aspects of practice.

The individualisation of patient care, along with the associated detailed documentation, has increased personal accountability for care delivery (Salvage 1995), However, individual professionals may have little control over different aspects of patients' experience making it difficult to ascertain where the actual accountability lies. This reinforces the importance of individual professionals maintaining clear and concise records of interventions so that it can easily be recognised who was responsible for what.

The Nursing and Midwifery Council (NMC) have provided clear guidance for record keeping and has acknowledged that good record keeping at an individual, team or organisational level helps to improve accountability (NMC 2009). They also emphasise that the principles of good record keeping apply to all types of records, regardless of the manner in which they are held. This principle is echoed by the Health Professions Council (HPC) who state that one of the duties of a registrant is to keep accurate records (HPC 2008).

Types of Accountability

Accountability is an individual responsibility. It is a crucial requirement for effective practice requiring you to think carefully about the decisions that you make and the actions that you take as a result of those decisions (Tee 2009).

Caulfield (2005) identified a framework which considers approaches based on four pillars of accountability that specify different types of authority in health care practice:

- Ethical,
- Legal,
- Professional,
- Employment.

Each of the four pillars of accountability will be considered below.

Ethical or moral accountability

An introduction to healthcare ethics was provided in Chapter 1; building on this it is important to emphasise that ethical values form part of the framework for accountability (Caulfield 2005). Health professionals are accountable to their patients and to each other for the ethical performance of their work (Wilkinson 2007) and must be cognisant with the ethical principles that guide their practice. Each professional will have gained personal ethical values from a number of different sources; these values will be drawn upon as part of the decision-making process.

Carper (1978) identified four 'ways of knowing' which make up the basic core of nursing knowledge: these include empirical knowledge, aesthetic knowledge (the art of nursing), personal knowledge and ethical knowledge. She recognised that ethical knowledge refers to knowledge of professional standards of conduct. Carper's analysis is applicable to all health professionals. As stated above, such standards are concerned with how a professional should act and are guided by basic moral principles and processes for determining right and wrong actions (Wilkinson 2007).

Nurses and other health professionals face ethical challenges in the provision of care on a daily basis (Ulrich et al. 2010) and it is crucial that they consider their ethical codes as guidelines for good professional practice. Meulenbergs et al. (2004) support this view and in addition argue that codes should be applied to allow for the increasing ethical demands associated with service delivery.

Legal accountability

For many years nurses were unaware of the fact that they were legally liable for their actions believing that ultimate liability rested with the organisation for which they worked. The meaning of professional accountability in the legal sense was recognised in the late 1970s (Clifford 1981). It is essential that all health professionals understand the legal implications of their work in order to protect themselves and their patients (Dimond 2012). As previously mentioned, society is becoming more litigious and as the number of legal cases in health care rises, it is crucial that all health professionals understand the legal accountability associated with their role. It is even more important when it is remembered that we are all presumed to know the law – ignorance is no excuse. This may seem to be an impossible standard. Health professionals must be prepared to seek advice if they are unsure of their position.

Caulfield (2005) stated that many nurses report that they are unclear about the impact that law has on their practice and that this can result in 'defensive nursing practice' and an unwillingness to put the needs of the client before the potential risk of legal implications. This undoubtedly applies to all health care professionals whatever their specialisation.

The key principles of law related to health care were outlined in Chapter 1 – where there has been a breach of the standard of care which the patient is entitled to expect, the patient may succeed in a legal action for damages for negligence. The issue of causation is especially difficult. You will remember that a link must be established between the breach of duty and the injury which has occurred. Without such a link there will be no liability for negligence. However, it must be remembered that even without such a link, the health care professional may still face action by the employer and/or the relevant professional governing body, placing employment and entitlement to practice at risk.

It should perhaps be added that in exceptional cases, the health care professional may incur criminal liability.

Professional accountability

Professional accountability is central to health care practice; it allows professionals to work within a framework for practice and to follow the principles identified by their professional body.

The general public must be able to trust the person who is caring for them; to justify that trust it is imperative that professionals adhere to a defined set of standards. The professional bodies, for example, the NMC and the HPC have clear expectations regarding the conduct of their registrants. The NMC Code (NMC 2008) provides the minimum standard of professional behaviour required from nurses and midwives; it emphatically states that 'as a professional, you are personally accountable for actions and omissions in your practice and must always be able to justify your decisions'. In parallel to this, the HPC Standards clearly state that 'as an autonomous and accountable professional, you need to make informed and reasonable decisions about your practice to make sure that you meet the standards that are relevant to your practice' (HPC 2008).

It is clear from the above examples that the professional bodies place the responsibility for safe practice firmly on you, as the qualified health professional.

Employment accountability – contracts with organisations

Each individual who is employed by an organisation will have a contract of employment which will detail the relationship that employee has with the employing organisation and set out the roles and responsibilities that are expected (Caulfield 2005). Within this contractual arrangement there will be clear guidance regarding an employee's accountability. Health professionals need to understand how their professional practice fits within the accountability framework of the organisation. This is of great importance to employers as the legal concept of vicarious liability means that an employer has legal responsibility even though the negligence causing the injury was solely due to the actions of the employee. The employer is liable to pay any compensation to which the injured party may be entitled. (For a more detailed discussion of the legal concept, see Chapter 1, pp. 11–12).

An important dimension of accountability for health professionals to consider stems from the governance structures within the organisation in which they work. Clinical Governance is central to a modern, patient-led health service and requires high levels of accountability for safe patient care (Tee 2009).

Allen (2001) suggests that clinical governance is a key development that has impacted on the contours of nursing work. Scally and Donaldson (1998: 61) define clinical governance as 'a system through which NHS organisations are accountable for continuously improving the quality of their services and safeguarding high standards of care by creating an environment in which excellence in clinical care will flourish'. The emphasis is on continuously improving the quality of patient care and developing the capacity of the NHS to maintain standards, including dealing with poor professional performance. This concept has implications for all health care professionals who are accountable for improving standards through the delivery of evidence-based care.

Accountability and Evidence-Based Practice

Historically health professionals have had a reputation for giving care that has been learnt through watching others and it has been argued that there was little empirical basis for the choice of intervention. The development of the empirical base of professional knowledge has gone a long way to dispel this attitude and health professionals are now recognised as delivering evidence-based care which is guided through robust clinical decisions.

Evidence-based practice may involve the whole health care team or it may be discipline specific. Research activity provides health professionals with the opportunity to use research findings to inform and influence their practice. However, it is important to emphasise that evidence can be identified from other sources, for example, clinical experience, quality improvement data even patient experiences. All health professionals are responsible for providing a high standard of practice that is informed through the best available evidence or best practice.

For at least three decades the importance of developing caring and respectful relationships with patients has been stressed and there has been a shift from task focused approaches to health care to an environment that responds to the holistic needs of individual patients. Along with this change in practice the importance of professional accountability has been increased resulting in a greater emphasis on the patient's experience through clinical effectiveness and evidence-based approaches to care (McCormack et al. 2004).

All health professionals are encouraged to take a step back and to reflect on their practice and on the services that they are providing (Lazenbatt 2002). It is crucial to question the evidence base for these services and ask whether they are efficient and effective. Evaluation needs to be carried out to inform professionals whether the service that they provide can be improved and this is an integral part of quality enhancement. Those involved in an evaluation process are accountable for providing evidence regarding how performance can be improved. Rycroft-Malone et al. (2004) highlight the importance of ensuring that the evidence used to inform practice (and policy) has been subject to scrutiny and Kitson et al. (1998) identified that the implementation of evidence-based practice is a complex process which is influenced by many factors.

Petrova et al. (2006) identified that the provision of health care is inseparable from universal values such as caring, helping and compassion. They noted that there has been an increasing consideration for individual values, particularly those of the patient. Further, they argue that such consideration is difficult within the context of modern health care, where complex and conflicting values are often in play. This is particularly so when a patient's values seem to be at odds with evidence-based practice or widely shared ethical principles, or when a health care professional's personal values may compromise the care provided.

Practice Development and Professional Accountability

There is an increasing emphasis on practice development in health care. This term has been used in relation to a range of activities which includes research, education and audit (Garbett & McCormack 2002). Regardless of how the term 'practice development' is interpreted, Garbett and McCormack (2004) identified that the main activities undertaken by professionals fell into the following categories:

- promoting and facilitating change,
- translation and communication,
- responding to external influences,
- education,
- facilitating the implementation of research into practice,
- audit and quality.

Arguably the main purpose of practice development and the focus for all of the above activities is increasing the effectiveness of patient-centred care. It must be recognised that for all health care professionals accountability is key to demonstrating the value of their contribution to the patients' journey. This is particularly relevant in terms of providing evidence of the quality of care that they provide and is reflected in Department of Health policy documents, for example, High quality care for all: NHS Next Stage Review final report (DH 2008).

All health professionals are accountable to themselves as well as to the organisation they work for. This is an important point, that is, whatever decision you take as a health professional you will have to live with this decision. Research on topics such as conscience (Jensen & Lidell 2009) and moral distress (see Chapter 9) suggest that professionals may experience guilt or even burnout if they do not do, what they consider to be, the right thing. An employing organisation will expect their employees to provide care that is clinically safe, efficient and effective (Kedge & Appleby 2009). Practice development is recognised as a key activity in moving practice on through the changing behaviours, values and beliefs of the staff involved (Garbett & McCormack 2002). All health professionals are responsible for keeping their knowledge and skills up-to-date and are accountable for delivering the best possible care for their patients. Failure to do so could lead to an allegation of negligence if the health professional causes injury/ damage because of out of date knowledge. This may seem to be impossibly harsh but the courts will take a reasonable approach as illustrated by the following case.

Crawford v Board of Governors of Charing Cross Hospital (1953 *The Times* 8 December, CA)

Mr Crawford suffered brachial palsy following an operation, allegedly because the anaesthetist has failed to take precautions in relation to the position of his arm.. An article had been published in The Lancet some six months prior to the operation drawing attention to the risk. It was the failure of the anaesthetist to read the article which allegedly amounted to negligence. The Court of Appeal held that the anaesthetist had not acted negligently: 'it would ... be putting too high a burden on a medical man to say that he has to read every article appearing in the current medical press; and it would be quite wrong to suggest that a medical man is negligent because he does not at once put into operation the suggestions [made]...' (per Lord Denning)

Application to Scenarios

The concept of accountability is pivotal to the two scenarios presented at the beginning of this chapter. As a professional you may already have given some thought to the questions posed regarding how you would respond and why.

A paramedic's predicament

If you were the paramedic in this situation, did you consider what you would need to know to make a decision that you could justify in terms of your ethical, legal and professional accountability? Also, what are the options that are open to you? Should the paramedic administer more analgesia?

Ethical issues

The ethical aspects of this scenario involve weighing up the potential benefits (principle of beneficence) and harms (non-maleficence) to the patient. You may like to revisit the discussion of ethical principles in Chapter 1. The patient is in 'severe pain' and there will need to be consideration of the need, and impact of, additional analgesia. The patient's autonomy also needs to be considered. If she has capacity (see Chapter 3 and 4) information will need to be provided about treatments offered, and alternatives, and consent obtained. The patient should also be consulted, where possible, regarding which family members or friends she wishes to be contacted and what information she wishes to be conveyed to them.

Legal issues

We have already seen that the paramedic, like any health professional, must act only within the limits of personal competence. The paramedic will have demonstrated competence in the delivery of pain relief whether by the use of opiates or other means. Failure to act competently may give rise to an allegation of negligence, the injury/damage resulting from the negligence being the 'unnecessarily prolonged' suffering of the patient.

In this scenario consideration needs to be given to the patient's condition – is it stable? how critical is the waiting time for the four by four vehicle? what pain relief can be given and what are the beliefs and rights of the patient? Some patients are very clear that they do not wish to be given morphine because they are concerned about issues such as addiction. It would be crucial to gain a patient's consent before administering any opiates. According to the *Misuse of Drugs Regulations 2001*, a paramedic may only be in possession of 20mg (see http://jrcalc.org.uk). More can be administered if it is available from another source.

Professional issues

Regarding the professional issues in this case, a clear conflict exists for the paramedic in this scenario. The HPC (2008) states that 'you must act in the best interests of service users' and adhere to your Scope of Practice. The paramedic would be expected to contact their control to ask for advice. The paramedic is carrying 20 mg morphine; however, a back up vehicle may also have a paramedic with another 20 mg. All paramedics should also have an alternative analgesia available such as Entonox.

Paramedics must have knowledge of the drug and its effects on the patient; they must be ready to respond to any side effect of administering morphine, for example, nausea and vomiting, hypotension and anaphylaxis. They need to ask themselves whether they have the equipment to cope with these possible outcomes. The paramedic should have checked that the ambulance carried Naloxone (Narcan), to reverse the effects and, ensured that Adrenaline is available in case of any adverse reactions.

It is important to emphasise that health care professionals must never act outside their professional competence (HPC 2008). There are national *guidelines* which *recommend* that a maximum dose of 20 mg morphine should be given (Joint Royal Colleges Ambulance Liaison Committee 2006) but these are not statutory requirements. Paramedics must always act in the best interests of their patients, provided this is demonstrably within their competence. Professionals must always obtain patient consent before administering a drug and must accept the fact that a patient may refuse an opiate- based analgesic because of their own particular view of that form of treatment.

Professionals must, on no account, make an uninformed decision because they feel pressured to respond to a situation. However, provided they have the competence to do so and can clinically justify their actions, registered paramedics may, on occasion, step beyond their clinical guidelines to act in the best interests of their patients.

Pressure to prescribe

The nurse prescriber in this scenario was acting under pressure and was persuaded to help out a colleague. She did not undertake the normal and required steps or precautions due to the time pressures and was therefore cutting corners and acting in an unsafe way. As a nurse in this scenario you would be accountable for your practice to patients, to your employer, to your professional body and to the law.

Ethical issues

The key ethical issues in this situation relate to the potential for, and the obligation to avoid, harm. Taking all steps necessary to avoid error and to ensure that professional practice benefits rather than harms patients is crucial. There is also an important ethical issue relating to truth telling (see Chapter 5) and the disclosure of error. Health professionals will, in situations like this, require courage to disclose their failings in the interests of patient well-being and safety. Their trustworthiness and integrity are at stake if they do not do so.

Legal issues

You will remember from the discussion in Chapter 1 that where there has been a breach of the standard of care which the patient is entitled to expect, the patient may succeed in legal action for damages for negligence. The patient will have to prove that the breach caused or materially contributed to the damage. The following case illustrates the problem faced by a patient who is unable to provide such proof.

Barnett v Chelsea and Kensington Hospital Management Committee QBD [1968] 1 All ER 1068

Mr B and 2 colleagues started vomiting after drinking some tea. They all went to the casualty department of the local hospital. The doctor who was called to attend by the nurse, was unwell and told the nurse to tell the men to go home to bed and call their own doctor if the vomiting continued. Mr B went home but died later that same

$\rightarrow$

day. The inquest found that he had died from arsenical poisoning – verdict murder by person or persons unknown. Mrs B did not succeed in her claim for damages for Mr B's death as the forensic evidence showed that Mr B would have died at the time that he did, even if he had been admitted to the hospital. The actions by the doctor did not in any way contribute to the death of Mr B.

There may be liability to compensate a victim of negligence when the action by the professional falls below the standard to be expected from a competent person undertaking the task. (You will remember that this is illustrated by the case of *Wilsher v Essex Area Health Authority* HL [1988] 1 All ER 871 which is discussed in Chapter 1.)

The primary legislation that enables nurses and midwives to prescribe is the *Medicinal Products: Prescription by Nurses and Others Act 1992*. Under this legislation it is clearly stated that prescribers must have sufficient knowledge and competence to undertake a thorough history of a patient, including medical history and medication history. In light of this it is clear that you, as the nurse, did not act competently. This is an example of unsafe prescribing as there is a breach in responsibility and accountability because the prescriber did not assess the patient. It is important to recognise that when professionals take on extended roles they should not become complacent and should always act within the competency framework associated with the role. That is, they should not undertake activities if they lack the necessary competence or confidence to conduct it safely.

As a prescriber you would be required to make decisions regarding the management of a patient's presenting condition and whether or not it is appropriate to prescribe any medication. You therefore would need to decide whether there are benefits associated with prescribing medication and if so you would need to advise the patient of the effects and risks and gain consent. The introduction of prescribing by nurses, midwives and other health professions such as pharmacists in 1992 was a new concept and it has taken a while to build public confidence in the role. Incidents such as the one described in the scenario are potentially very damaging as they could reduce the general public's confidence in health care professionals, other than doctors, prescribing medication.

This situation could have been prevented if you, as the nurse, had acted competently, adhered to the foundations of accountability and had not cut corners in the prescribing process. It is recognised that medication errors can occur at any point in the process of prescribing and administering medications. All individuals engaged in the prescription and administration of medications must therefore be vigilant and must always adhere to the relevant guidelines.

Professional issues

The professional issues in relation to this scenario relate to the importance of understanding the standards established by the professional regulators in respect of additional qualifications. The NMC, for example, has published clear Standards (NMC 2006) to prepare nurses and midwives to prescribe. These should be adhered to at all times. As a qualified nurse or non-medical prescriber you would be responsible for checking Mrs Banks' allergy status and you should have known not to prescribe without assessing the patient first. The nurse administering the drug should have checked the patients' allergy status and should also have a good knowledge of the generic and the trade names for medication; this would have alerted her to the fact that Mrs Banks was allergic to Metoclopramide as Maxalon is the trade name for this particular medication.

As a qualified nurse prescriber the standard of care that you provide would be expected to exceed that given by a first level qualified nurse and it is also expected that you accept a higher level of accountability (Childs et al. 2009). It is also clear from the scenario that there was a communication problem as information from the patient's notes had not been transferred onto the current drug chart. There is the potential in a situation like this for the professional's actions and omissions to compromise the well-being of the patient and to undermine standards of practice. The need to 'be open and honest and act with integrity' (NMC 2008) makes the obligation to disclose error clear and imperative.

In a situation like this, a nurse prescriber should have completed a thorough assessment of the patient to include a check of her allergy status. Medication errors are a real threat to patient safety and the event that has been described in the scenario would be seen as a preventable incident. An adverse drug reaction must always be reported as soon as possible and actions taken by all parties must be clearly identified. Events such as this should be used as an opportunity for learning.

The National Patient Safety Agency (NPSA) was set up in 2001 to improve patient safety. One way in which this is achieved is through encouraging professionals to report adverse incidents and near misses as improving safety requires staff to acknowledge and learn from mistakes (NPSA 2004). The adverse event which occurred in respect of Mrs Banks could have been avoided if a similar incident had taken place and learning had occurred as a result of analysing the actions which led to the error being made.

Conclusion

It is clear from the previous discussions that all health professionals must be aware that they are accountable ethically, legally and professionally in their daily practice. There has been a growing emphasis on both individual and organisational accountability which has occurred in parallel with the general public's increasing knowledge of the legal basis of the professional/patient relationship.

All health professionals must be cognisant of and adhere to their code of professional conduct to ensure that they act appropriately to protect themselves and their patients. Codes of practice must be continuously reviewed to make sure that they are fit for purpose and provide registrants with the ethical and legal framework to guide their practice.

Acknowledgements

The author acknowledges input from Claire Palles-Clark and Verity Snook who suggested the case examples and advised on the discussion. We would also like to thank Malcolm Woollard who provided guidance regarding paramedic practice.

References

Allen, D. (2001) *The Changing Shape of Nursing Practice* Routledge, London.

Carper, B. (1978) Fundamental patterns of knowing in nursing. *Advances in Nursing Science* 1 13–123.

Caulfield, H. (2005) *Accountability: Vital Notes for Nurses*. Blackwell Publishing. Oxford.

Childs, L., Coles, L. & Marjoram B. (Eds) (2009) *Essential Skills Clusters for Nurses Theory for Practice*. Wiley-Blackwell, Chichester.

Clifford, J.C. (1981) Managerial control versus professional autonomy: a paradox. *Journal of Nursing Administration*, 11, 19–21.

Department of Health (2008) *High quality care for all: NHS Next Stage Review final report*. Department of Health, London.

Dimond, B. (2012) *Legal Aspects of Nursing* (6th ed.). Pearson Education Limited, Essex.

Garbett, R. & McCormack, B. (2002) A concept analysis of practice development. *Journal of Research in Nursing*, 7(2), 87–100.

Health Professions Council (2008) *Standards of Conduct, Performance and Ethics*. HPC, London.

Hood, L.J. & Pepper, S.K. (2006) *Leddy and Pepper's Conceptual Bases of Professional Nursing*. Lippincott Williams and Wilkins, Philadelphia.

Jensen, A. & Lidell, E. (2009) The influence of conscience in nursing. *Nursing Ethics*, 16(1), 31–42.

Joint Royal Colleges Ambulance Liaison Committee (2006) Clinical practice guidelines updates post 2006 publication of the UK Ambulance Service Clinical Practice Guidelines accessed 14 December 2010.

Joint Royal Colleges Ambulance Liaison Committee (2011) *Misuse of Drugs Regulations 2001*, http://jrcalc. org.uk/paramedics_g1.pdf, accessed 20 May 2011.

Kedge, S. & Appleby, B. (2009) Promoting a culture of curiosity within nursing practice. British *Journal of Nursing*, 18(10), 6–68.

Kitson, A., Harvey, G., & McCormack, B. (1998) Enabling the implementation of evidence based practice: a conceptual framework. *Quality in Health Care* 7, 149–158.

Lazenbatt, A. (2002) *The Evaluation Handbook for Health care professionals*. Roulledge, London.

McCormack, B., Manley, K. & Garbett, R. (Eds) (2004) *Practice Development in Nursing*. Blackwell, Oxford.

Medicinal Products: Prescription by Nurses and Others Act (1992) Gov. UK.

Meulenbergo, T., Vorpreet, E., Schotsmans, P. & Gastmans, C. (2004) Professional codes in a changing nursing context: literature review. *Journal of Advanced Nursing*, 46(3), 331–336

National Patient Safety Agency (2004) *Seven Steps to Patient Safety*. NPSA, London.

Nursing and Midwifery Council (2006) *Standards of Proficiency for Nurse and Midwife Prescribers*. NMC, London.

Nursing and Midwifery Council (2008) *The Code: Standards of Conduct, Performance and Ethics for Nurses and Midwives*. NMC, London.

Nursing and Midwifery Council (2009) *Record Keeping: Guidance for Nurses and Midwives*. NMC, London.

Petrova, M., Dale, J. & Fulford, B. (2006) Values-based practice in primary care: easing the tensions between individual values, ethical principles and best evidence. *British Journal of General Practice*, 56(530), 703–709.

Rycroft-Malone, J., Seers, K., Titchen, A., Harvey, G., Kitson, A. & McCormack, B. (2004) What counts as evidence in evidence-based practice? *Journal of Advanced Nursing*, 47(1), 81–90.

Salvage, J. (1995) Political implications of the named-nurse concept. *Nursing Times*, 91 (41), 36–37.

Scally, G. & Donaldson, L.J. (1998) Clinical governance and the drive for quality improvement in the new NHS in England. *British Medical Journal*, 317(7150), 61–65.

Tee, S.R. (2009) 'Ethical and Legal Principles for Health care' in Childs, L.L., Coles, L. & Marjoram, B. (Eds) *Essential Skills Clusters for Nurses: Theory for Practice*. Wiley-Blackwell, West Sussex.

Ulrich, C.M., Taylor, C., Soeken, K., O'Donnell, P., Farrar, A., Danis, M. & Grady, C. (2010) Everyday ethics: ethical issues and stress in nursing practice. *Journal of Advanced Nursing*, 66(11).

Wilkinson, J.M. (2007) *Nursing Process and Critical Thinking* (4th ed.). Pearson, New Jersey.

Chapter 3

Informed consent:
adults with capacity

Kevin Acott and Steve Searby

Consent is one of the cornerstones of ethical healthcare practice and research. Although the concept is ancient, dating back to the beginnings of the common law, its importance has increased in response to violations of human rights in medical experimentation over the last century. Today, there is an acute awareness of the importance of consent in healthcare. Professionals have privileged access to the bodies, thoughts and medical information of patients. In everyday practice, you are likely to touch patients to record blood pressure, to help them to wash and dress, to insert intravenous lines for fluids and medication and to share information with their relatives. Patients are vulnerable to physical, emotional and psychological harm and need to be both protected and informed. Without the consent of the patients, activities that involve touching or sharing patient information may be unethical, illegal and unprofessional.

The ethical, legal and professional aspects of consent are complex and require an understanding of concepts such as autonomy, trespass, capacity, paternalism and the right to refuse. The tort of negligence is also very relevant particularly in the context of the information which must be given before consent can be valid.

This chapter focuses on consent to care, treatment and research in healthcare when patients have capacity. It explores the everyday aspects of consent as they might arise in your own practice. The next chapter (Chapter 4) explores aspects of consent when patient capacity is compromised or lacking.

We begin with two scenarios that invite you to reflect on consent issues and to consider responses that are ethical, legal and professional.

Aspects of consent will then be explored and an analysis of the scenarios will follow later in the chapter.

As you read the scenarios we suggest that you have two questions in mind:

- ▶ If you were the professional, what would you do?
- ▶ Why would you respond this way? Refer to relevant ethical, legal and professional concepts and arguments that could support your action.

Scenarios

 A consent dilemma for an operating department professional

Adam, aged 25, has been admitted to hospital to have a cystoscopy, an elective surgical procedure, as he has been having recurrent bladder problems. Adam, in consultation with his wife and consultant surgeon, has signed a consent form previously for the procedure. From the admitting ward he is taken to theatre where consent is again checked with the theatre team. He is then given a general anaesthetic in the anaesthetic room. Now anaesthetised and asleep he is moved into the operating theatre.

However, as soon as the surgical team started, it rapidly becomes apparent that to gain access to the bladder Adam would need to have a circumcision. His wife is informed of this and she decides that she wants the surgical team to go ahead with the procedure. She argues that as it is deemed necessary to be able to get into the bladder then it is better for her husband to have both procedures done at the same time. You are the operating department professional and the surgeon discusses the situation with you and other members of the team. He asks for your opinion regarding the right course of action.

A nurse's response to non-attendance for depot injection

Patrick is a 35 year old man diagnosed with schizophrenia who receives depot Risperidone injections on a monthly basis. You are the practice nurse at a general practitioner's (GP's) surgery. Patrick has been receiving medication by injection for about fifteen years and has not been in direct contact with a mental health team for five years. At Patrick's last visit two months ago, you observed that he appeared well and that the medication seems to be helping him maintain a reasonably satisfying lifestyle. He has not arrived for his appointment today and you have not had a message from him. He has done this before but has always returned the following month.

Informed Consent: Background and Meaning

An oft quoted acknowledgment of the importance of consent was made by Judge Cardoza, in the US case of *Schloendorff* v *Society of New York Hospital* 105 NE 92 (NY, 1914) when he stated:

> Every human being of adult years and sound mind has a right to determine what shall be done with his body; and a surgeon who performs an operation without his patient's consent commits an assault.

The first clear statement of consent requirements in healthcare ethics appeared in the Nuremberg Code in 1947. This was in response to the abuse and murder of children and adults in the concentration camps during the Nazi era. The exploitation and disregard for human rights and life was presented as 'medical research' (Manson & O'Neill 2007: 2–3). The term 'informed consent' did not, however, appear until the 1950s and did not receive serious attention until the 1970s (Beauchamp & Childress 2009: 117). The focus of informed consent was initially on research, however, it soon became recognised that this was also an important concept in relation to healthcare activities. In the USA patients have a right to accept or decline interventions and to have all the information about the proposed treatment, including any risks attached to the treatment, which they need to make an informed choice.

In the United Kingdom, the courts take a slightly different view. In order to give a valid consent the patient must have been given the information necessary to enable a decision to be made in the full exercise of autonomy. A real difficulty is to decide exactly what and how much information should be given to the patient. There have been a number of recent cases in which the judges have tried to clarify this issue. The first modern case considering this issue is *Sidaway*, details of which appear below.

Sidaway v Bethlem Royal Hospital Governors HL [1985] 1 All ER 643

Mrs S underwent an operation on her cervical vertebrae performed by a neurosurgeon. However skilfully the operation was performed there was a 1 to 2 per cent risk of damage to the nerve root at the site of the operation or to the spinal cord. There was no negligence in the way the operation was performed but Mrs S suffered damage to her spinal cord leaving her with severe ill effects. She alleged that the surgeon had been negligent in that he had not informed her of the risk of such damage. The claim for damages was dismissed. Lord Scarman explained the extent of the duty to disclose elements of risk, saying:

> ...English law must recognise a duty of the doctor to warn his patient of risk inherent in the treatment which he is proposing.... The critical limitation is that the duty is confined to material risk. [The test of whether a risk is material] is whether ... a reasonable person in the patient's position would be likely to attach significance to the risk.

It would be understandable if you found Lord Scarman's explanation somewhat obscure. Other judges have tried to clarify the requirement in a number of later cases. In one such case, Lord Woolf MR said:

> If there is a significant risk which would affect the judgment of the reasonable patient, then in the normal course it is the responsibility of a doctor to inform the patient of that significant risk, if the information is needed so that the patient can determine for him or herself as to what course he or she should adopt. (*Pearce v United Bristol Healthcare NHS Trust (1998) 48 BMLR 11*)

This still leaves the professional to decide when and what information should be given. Lord Steyn put it another way:

> A surgeon owes a legal duty to a patient to warn him or her in general terms of possible serious risks involved in the procedure. ... In modern law medical paternalism no longer rules and a patient has a prima facie right to be informed ... of a small, but well established, risk of serious injury. (*Chester v Ashfar [2004] UKHL 41* at para. 16)

As a result of judicial decisions, the concept of informed consent, although not described as such, has taken root in a modified way in the United Kingdom. It seems that it is still a matter for the judgment of the professional to decide what risks should be disclosed but there is no longer any doubt that the patient has the right to be given all information needed to inform a decision. The Bolam test (discussed in Chapter 1) will be applied so that the health professional gives such information as a responsible body of opinion believes to be appropriate.

Elements of Consent

In your everyday practice in healthcare you may sometimes doubt if the steps taken to obtain consent are adequate. Beauchamp and Childress (2009: 120) suggest that:

One gives an informed consent to an intervention if (and perhaps only if) one is competent to act, receives a thorough disclosure, comprehends the disclosure, acts voluntarily, and consents to the intervention.

There are, therefore, at least five elements that need to be considered:

- Competence,
- Disclosure,
- Understanding,
- Voluntariness,
- Consent.

We will discuss each of these elements to illustrate the implications for practice.

Competence – a patient must understand and make a decision regarding the particular intervention. In the UK, the focus is now on mental capacity, a concept which focuses on decision-making capability in relation to specific circumstances. More will be said about this in the discussion of the legal aspects of consent below and also in Chapter 4.

Disclosure – the legal duty to inform the patient has already been discussed but more practical explanation is undoubtedly needed. In considering what and how much information to share with a patient, you may ask what you would like to know if you were in the same position. Generally, disclosure will involve explaining what the intervention is and why it is being considered for this patient. You need also to share the nature of the intervention; for example, if it is a surgical procedure you will need to explain how and where it will happen, who will do the procedure, how long it will take, what the risks and benefits are and what alternatives there are.

If the patient is being approached about participation in a research project, additional information will be necessary. This information will be presented on a Participant Information Sheet written so it is understandable to the potential research participants. Information relating to confidentiality will need to be included with responses to questions such as: will the data obtained during the study be anonymised (you can read more about confidentiality in Chapter 6) and how will the researcher respond if there is evidence of actual or potential harm to an individual? Potential participants will also need to be made aware of expenses that may be offered, who they can complain to if they are unhappy with the conduct of the research and whether a lay summary of findings will be available.

Understanding – there are many possible factors that determine how much or how little information is understood by patients or research participants. Factors that may influence understanding may include the clarity of information provided, the nature of the health condition, language difficulties, anxiety or fear or perhaps level of maturity or education. The health professional's role is to ensure that necessary information is presented clearly and that patients have time to consider it and ask questions about areas they are uncertain of . If the patient's first language is not English it may be necessary to use the services of an interpreter. To check the understanding of patients or potential research participants, they should be asked to say what they understand of the information that has been shared with them. Should patients tell you that they have not understood the information from another professional, then it is advisable to contact the latter and suggest they return to discuss the patient's queries.

Voluntariness – for this condition to be met during the consent process, patients must not be subjected to factors which might influence their decision. There are different ways that a patient or research participant may be influenced, compromising ability to make autonomous decisions during the consent process. Certain influences are not acceptable:

- ▶ Coercion involves the use or threat of harm or force to control another person. An example would be if a health professional told a patient that he or she will be forcibly taken to a mental health unit if medication is refused.
- ▶ Persuasion may involve the use of reason to influence a patient's decision. If a health professional provides reasons for hospital admission accepted by the patient as reasonable this could be described as persuasion. It needs to be remembered that different reasons may influence different individuals.
- ▶ Manipulation involves getting people to do what someone else wants through persuasion or coercion. It may involve deception whereby information is exaggerated, withheld or distorted to lead the person to do what the other person wants. An example might be a situation where a health professional suggests to a patient who wishes to leave a dementia care unit, that the family is on holiday or that transport is not available, when these explanations are untrue.

Consent – This involves a patient's decision to agree to and authorise any aspect of healthcare intervention, such as surgery or blood transfusion, or participation in a research project. For most healthcare interventions, verbal consent is adequate and written consent would not be considered necessary. However, for interventions with more potential for harm and for research, written consent is required.

Rationale for Consent

It seems undeniable that issues of consent will always be crucial in healthcare. In all areas of practice, situations emerge in which a patient may or may not choose to allow a professional to do something to him or her. The overall rationale for consent in healthcare is to protect patients and research participants from unwanted interventions and from coercion, abuse and exploitation. Understanding the ethical, legal and professional issues underpinning consent is an important requirement of professional accountability as discussed in Chapter 1.

Ethical aspects

There has been a change in healthcare practice in recent years. The shift has been from 'paternalistic traditions, in which professionals were seen as the proper judges of patients' best interests' (O'Neill 2002: 2) to respect for patients' autonomy and rights. As O'Neill (ibid) puts it:

> Increased recognition and respect for patients' rights and insistence on the ethical importance of securing their consent are now viewed as standard and obligatory ways of securing respect for patients' autonomy.

Although the principle of respect for autonomy is most commonly cited as supporting consent, other principles are also relevant. Johnstone (2004: 141) reminds us that the four principles relate to consent as follows:

- Autonomy – 'which demands respect for patients as self-determining choosers, and justifies allowing them the option of accepting risks'.
- Non-maleficence – 'which demands the protection of patients from battery, assault, trespass, exploitation and other harms that may result from inadequate or inappropriate consent processes (including the inadequate or inappropriate disclosure of information'.

- Beneficence – 'which demands the maximisation of patient well-being via consent processes.' There is much potential for benefit and harm from healthcare interventions and research. The well-being and interests of individuals need to be the main consideration during the informationgiving and consent process. If benefits and harms or risks are uncertain this needs to be made clear. It must also be made clear, if this is the case, that a research intervention or study is more likely to benefit future patients rather than research participants.
- Justice – 'which demands fairness and that patients not be unduly or intolerably burdened by consent processes'. Justice would also include not depriving people of the opportunity to participate in research if they wished. This also involves balancing the right to protection and the right to participate.

Legal aspects

In law, any touching of a person without consent or other lawful justification may give rise to a civil action for trespass on the person which may take a number of different forms:

- **Assault** – something which makes a person apprehend that he/she is about to be touched, for example being approached by a health professional carrying a hypodermic needle;
- **Battery** – actually touching a person;
- **False imprisonment** – preventing persons from leaving the place where they are.

In each case, the patient's consent, or the authority of law (compulsory detention for treatment under the provisions of the *Mental Health Act 1983* as amended), will be a complete defence to any legal action.

There may also be criminal liability for assault, although this is unlikely in the general context of the delivery of healthcare.

Dimond (2012), discussing the tort of 'trespass to the person' suggests that to maintain dignity and respect, to protect ourselves and our patients/clients and to prevent possible litigation, it is imperative that consent is obtained. For health professionals, the relationship between a patient and the professional must be 'patient-centred', based on trust, respect and dignity. Dimond (2012) and DH (2009) state that 'consent' must be given voluntarily without duress or undue influence, by a mentally competent person who has been suitably informed.

There are three conditions that must be satisfied for consent to be legally effective:

- The patient must have capacity to make the decision (see Re C *(Adult: Refusal of Treatment) [1994] 1 WLR 290 (FD)* discussed in detail later in this chapter at p. 55);
- The person must understand the nature and purpose of the act;
- The decision must be voluntary that is free from coercion and undue influence. However, there is a difference between coercion and reassurance; a patient who is simply told to take the medicine may feel under pressure to obey the professional, that is coerced, while a patient who is told that if the medicine is taken, this is likely to lead to improvement may feel re-assured.

(These conditions are discussed in more detail above under the heading 'Elements of Consent' at p. 47.)

Legally there is no specific requirement regarding how consent is given. What is of concern is evidence of consent having been given. As discussed above, consent can be given in a number of ways and these are:

- Word of mouth;
- Implied;
- In writing.

You may be aware from your healthcare experience, a professional or a patient, that consent may be given in each of these forms.

Verbal consent is self-explanatory; a simple 'Yes' or 'No' will suffice to convey agreement or refusal. An accurate record is essential.

Implied consent (also referred to as presumed or tacit consent) occurs when by his/her action the patient consents to the proposed treatment, for example, on approaching a patient to take his/her blood pressure he/she may raise an arm and not require an explanation or a formal request; by this action the patient is consenting to blood pressure being taken and recorded. Although it may not seem necessary, good practice requires that you do provide information about the procedure you are about to conduct and gain the patient's consent. Again an accurate record must be made containing sufficient detail to justify the conclusion reached that consent can be implied.

In relation to verbal and implied consent both the Nursing and Midwifery Council's (NMC) Standards (2008) and the Standards (2008) published by the Health Professions Council (HPC) require health professionals to maintain accurate records.

Written consent is self-explanatory; the patient signs a document which records that consent is given. You may have observed a consultant talk to a patient about a surgical procedure, providing information and asking for a consent form to be signed. In many areas, patients are approached to participate in research with the aim of assessing the impact of different interventions, such as medication. If you have witnessed this, you will have noticed that the patients, as potential research participants, are provided with an information sheet (Participant Information Sheet), offered opportunities to ask questions and given time to consider whether they participate in the research or not. The latter two situations are examples when *explicit consent* is sought. Consent is then given orally or in writing. The legal validity of these different forms of consent will be discussed below.

Written consent would seem to be the best form of consent as patients sign to indicate agreement with the procedure or treatment. It is even then essential that the patient has sufficient understanding of the procedure, that the benefits and risks have been explained and if there are any alternative choices, these must be presented to allow patients to make an informed choice, acting autonomously. Failure to ensure that the criteria are met, can mean that the patient alleges negligence by the professional on the basis that consent would not have been given had the patient been properly informed.

Consent remains valid for a reasonable time unless:

▶ It is withdrawn by the patient which may happen at any time – patients with capacity have an absolute right to change their mind
▶ New information becomes available which may indicate that the original consent might be invalid, for example, if it becomes known that there has been undue influence. This is a question of fact as illustrated by the following case.

Re T [1992] 4 All ER 649

T was raised as a Jehovah's Witness but had not taken membership as an adult. She was involved in a car accident which left her needing a →

blood transfusion. After her mother had been to see her, T said that she refused any blood transfusion. Her boyfriend and her father claimed that T had been subjected to pressure by her mother.

The Court of Appeal held that consent would be negated if the will of the patient had been overwhelmed by pressure from someone else, in this case T's mother.

▶ Evidence of risks or new treatment options become available or the patient's condition changes significantly between the time when consent was sought and when the intervention is undertaken. In both situations the professional should draw the patient's attention to the changes and obtain consent in the light of such changes. (DoH *Reference Guide to consent for examination or treatment* (2nd ed) July 2009, para. 42)

Professional aspects

The Nursing and Midwifery Council's (NMC) Standards (2008) and the Standards (2008) published by the Health Professions Council (HPC) both require a professional to obtain consent before beginning any treatment or care.

Section 9 of the HPC Code (2008: 11) states:

▶ You must get informed consent to give treatment (except in an emergency)

▶ You must explain to the patient, client or user the treatment you are planning on carrying out, the risks involved and any other treatments possible. You must make sure that you get their informed consent to any treatment you do carry out.

▶ You must make a record of the person's treatment decision and pass this on to all members of the health and social-care team involved in the care.

▶ In emergencies, you may not be able to explain treatment, get consent or pass on information to other members of the health or social-care team. However, you should still try to do all of these things as far as you can.

▶ If someone refuses treatment and you believe that it is necessary for their well-being, you must make reasonable efforts to persuade them, particularly if you think that there is a significant or immediate risk to their life.

▶ You must keep to your employers' procedures on consent and be aware of any guidance issues by the Department of Health or other appropriate authority in the country in which you practise.

The NMC Code (2008, paras 13–17) states that you must:

▶ You must ensure you gain consent before you begin any treatment or care.
▶ You must respect people's rights to accept or decline treatment or care.
▶ You must uphold people's rights to be fully involved in decisions about their care.
▶ You must be aware of the legislation regarding mental capacity, ensuring that people who lack capacity remain at the centre of decision-making and are fully safeguarded.
▶ You must be able to demonstrate that you have acted in someone's best interests if you have provided care in an emergency.

The patient's right to make an autonomous decision to consent to or refuse the proposed treatment and to have that autonomous choice respected is upheld by both Codes.

Remember that breach of the Codes may lead to disciplinary action by the NMC or HPC unless departure from the Code can be justified in the specific circumstances of that particular patient.

Obtaining Consent

Consent must be obtained by the person undertaking the clinical procedure. A health professional must not gain consent on behalf of another person. Consent is an ongoing process rather than a one-off event, and it should be sought before the procedure starts. Health professionals need to ensure that patients are offered more than one opportunity to consent to or refuse an intervention. Consent should also be sought before surgery and in good time, for example, before a pre-med medication before surgery is given, otherwise the validity of the consent could be questioned, and once again check before the procedure starts. In addition to the individual Codes/Standards of Practice, the Department of Health publishes guidance on consent issues.

Introducing Mental Capacity (Competence) and Consent

The *Mental Capacity Act 2005* (as amended) states 'A person must be assumed to have capacity unless it is established that he lacks capacity.' s. 1(2) The Act sets out the requirements which must be observed for patients who lack capacity and is dealt with in more detail in the next chapter. Case law establishes that the presence of a mental disorder does not automatically preclude the person from making a valid decision in relation to treatment. This is illustrated by the case described below.

Re C (Adult: Refusal of Medical Treatment) [1994] 1 All ER 819

C was an elderly gentleman diagnosed with paranoid schizophrenia, and had been a resident in Broadmoor psychiatric hospital for more than 30 years. He had developed a gangrenous foot. It was decided by the clinicians that the appropriate treatment for his condition was amputation of the foot. C refused consent stating he would rather die with all four limbs than live with only three. Thorpe j granted an injunction to prevent amputation on the basis that C was able to understand and retained the relevant information, believed it and had arrived at a clear choice.

The necessity to accept a decision by a patient with capacity which the professional believes to be unwise or irrational can be difficult for the professional. This was illustrated when a 22-year-old mother died just hours after giving birth to twins, because doctors were not allowed to give a blood transfusion to her, as she was a Jehovah's Witness (Attewill 2007). Complications had arisen following the birth which required an immediate transfusion. Despite the medical team explaining the consequences of not having treatment, the patient refused the blood because of her religious beliefs. As a capable adult, the patient was able to refuse treatment and the medical team had to accept her decision, even though the consequences were that the patient died. Therefore, if a patient who has mental capacity refuses medical treatment and even after the nurse explains the requirement for it, if the patient still refuses, there is nothing the nurse can do. If the patient were to be coerced into accepting the treatment, then this would invalidate the consent.

Application to Scenarios

It has been said that consent is one of the cornerstones of ethical and legal healthcare practice and research (see http://www.nhs.uk). Two scenarios were outlined at the beginning of this chapter with two questions. You are now invited to revisit the scenarios and the questions:

▶ If you were the professional, what would you do?
▶ Why would you respond this way? Refer to relevant ethical, legal and professional issues that could support your decision and action.

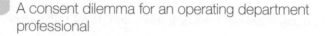 A consent dilemma for an operating department professional

After discussion with the hospital trust lawyer, it was decided not to proceed with the circumcision. The patient had a right to make his own decision and could have gone to litigation if procedure had been done against his will. However, during this time when the arguments were being presented, Adam was kept anaesthetised and asleep in the Operating Theatre. Subsequently Adam was woken up and sent back to the ward to be admitted another day.

Ethical issues

In this scenario it is necessary to consider how the relevant ethical principles apply. In informed consent situations, where the patient has capacity, the principle of respect for autonomy is likely to trump other principles. However, in this case Adam is anaesthetised and is unable to express his view regarding the additional procedure. The procedure is not in the context of an emergency situation and a consideration of beneficence and non-maleficence supports waiting until Adam is able to make a decision for himself. The delay may be inconvenient as the procedure will need to be re-scheduled but it is preferable to conducting a procedure that the patient has not consented to and may object to.

Legal issues

As we have seen, consent is needed before any treatment can legally be carried out. In Adam's case that consent was limited to the cystoscopy. To continue with the circumcision would mean a procedure being undertaken to which Adam had not consented. Unless the clinical situation is such that the procedure needs to be done as a matter of urgency, and as Adam has capacity when awake, it is right to wait for his decision. As Adam temporarily lacks capacity, the surgeon has to decide whether or not Adam's best interests require him to continue the surgery.

Professional issues

The NMC Code (2008) at paragraphs 13–17 and the HPC Code (2008) at paragraph 9 emphasise the duty to ensure the participation of patients in decisions about their care except in cases of emergency.

A nurse's response to non-attendance for depot injection

Two weeks after Patrick's non-attendance, Jo the Practice Nurse receives a phone call from Patrick's mother saying she is concerned as he has been acting 'oddly'. She said he appears to be troubled by voices and has been walking round the family garden naked late at night. The Practice Nurse suggests that Patrick is encouraged to come to the surgery to discuss the way forward. The next day Patrick comes to see the Practice Nurse. He tells her that he is well and does not need to continue medication. The Practice Nurse takes the time to find out why Patrick has reached this conclusion and begins by asking how he has been feeling. He admits that he has not been feeling well and has been troubled by hearing voices that prevent him from sleeping and instruct him to do unusual things. Jo asks how he was when he was having his depot regularly. Patrick admits that he has not understood the role of the medication in his recovery. Jo provides Patrick with information about his depot injection. She outlines the benefits, risks and alternative treatments. Patrick had tried a range of treatments before he began regular depot injections. He agreed that this had kept him stable and he had, until recently, managed to work regularly. Jo explains the importance of maintaining medication in keeping distressing symptoms under control. Realising that Patrick may have felt unsupported, Jo reassures him that more help will be made available to him. Patrick agrees to maintain the medication on the basis that help is readily available to enable him to talk through his concerns.

Ethical issues

There are many reasons why people who experience mental distress withdraw from treatment. Failure to comply with medication may be due to three themes (see Gurney 2004: 722):

▶ **The person** – their values, experiences and lifestyle. If, for example, the patient is homeless or takes non-prescribed drugs such as cannabis and alcohol this may effect compliance;

▶ **The illness** – thought disorder or depression may influence ability to comply. If a patient is hearing voices, for example, he or she may be preoccupied or take the view that professionals are not trustworthy and to be avoided;

▶ **The treatment** – whether the relationship with the professional is considered positive by patients is an important aspect of compliance. Do they, for example, feel respected and listened to? Has the treatment been explained and do the benefits outweigh the side-effects?

Sound ethical practice (supported by NICE Guidelines) tells us that, unless a patient clearly lacks capacity, he or she has the right to refuse medication: the principles of 'concordance' (an informed, negotiated agreement between professional and patient) or informed 'adherence' are key here:

> Addressing non-adherence is not about getting patients to take more medicines per se. Rather, it starts with an exploration of patients' perspectives of medicines and the reasons why they may not want or are unable to use them. Health professionals have a duty to help patients make informed decisions about treatment and use appropriately prescribed medicines to best effect. (NICE 2009: 8)

Responding ethically to a patient in a situation such as this requires consideration of the factors that make compliance difficult. An ethical response involves taking time, listening and responding honestly to patient questions and concerns. It should not be assumed that just because a person has a mental health diagnosis that he or she lacks capacity (justice). Rather, the focus should be on forming an alliance , respecting the autonomy of patients, working with them to maintain wellness. Building a trusting relationship requires openness and honesty regarding the benefits (beneficence) and risks or disadvantages (non-maleficence) of different approaches to treatment and care.

Legal issues

If the situation had escalated with Patrick progressing from acting 'oddly' to becoming aggressive compromising his own safety and the safety of his family, action could be taken using the *Mental Health Act 1983 (as amended)* resulting in compulsory admission to hospital for assessment/treatment. To rely solely on the 'threat of being sectioned' to gain agreement to have the medication could be argued to be coercive and thus to negate his consent. The Practice Nurse has been able to reassure Patrick and as a result he has given a valid consent.

Professional issues

The NMC Code (2008) at paragraphs 13–17 and the HPC Code (2008) at paragraph 9 emphasise the duty of a health professional to ensure the participation of patients in decisions and to acknowledge the patient's right to consent or refuse treatment. There is a duty to inform the patient of any significant risks of refusal – in this scenario, the risk of compulsory admission to hospital under 'section'.

Conclusion

As a health professional you have privileged access to the bodies of patients and information about them. There is also potential for the development of collaborative, respectful relationships with patients. Failure to understand and practice in accord with the requirements of informed consent gives rise to the possibility of disrespect, abuse and exploitation of the patient.

This chapter has provided opportunities for you to consider scenarios from practice where professionals provide information so that patients can make informed decisions about their care and treatment. This is likely to require time, a willingness to engage authentically with patients and to utilise excellent communication skills. The investment is worthwhile to ensure, as far as possible, that patients receive the care and treatment they need. It is also necessary to ensure that you engage with informed consent ethically, legally and professionally. The next chapter enables you to understand the informed consent process when patient capacity is compromised.

References

Allewlll, F. (2007) Jehovah's Witness mother dies after refusing blood transfusion. *The Guardian*. 5 May 2007.

Beauchamp, T.L. & Childress, J.F. (2009) *Principles of Biomedical Ethics* (6th ed.). University Press Oxford, Oxford.

Department of Health (2009) *Reference Guide to Consent for Examination or Treatment*, (2nd ed.). HMSO, London.

Dimond, B.C. (2012) *Legal Aspects of Nursing* (6th ed.). Pearson Education, Harlow.

Gurney, S. (2004) 'Medication management to concordance' in Norman, I. & Ryrie, I. (Eds) *The Art and Science of Mental Health Nursing: A Textbook of Principles and Practice*. Open University Press, Maidenhead, pp. 719–728.

Health Professions Council (2008) *Standards of Conduct, Performance and Ethics*. HPC, London.

Johnstone, M-J. (2004) *Bioethics: A Nursing Perspective* (4th ed.). Churchill Livingstone, Sydney.

Manson, N.C. & O'Neill, O. (2007) *Rethinking Informed Consent in Bioethics*. Cambridge University Press, Cambridge.

National Health Service, http://www.nhs.uk/conditions/ Consent-to-treatment/Pages/ Introduction.aspx Accessed 30 May 2011.

National Institute for Health and Clinical Excellence (2009) NICE *Guideline 76: Medicines Adherence: Involving patients in decisions about prescribed medicines and supporting adherence*. NICE, London.

Nursing and Midwifery Council (2008) *The Code, Standards for Performance, Conduct and Ethics*. NMC, London.

O'Neill, O. (2002) *Autonomy and Trust in Bioethics*. Cambridge University Press, Cambridge.

Chapter 4

Consent when capacity is compromised

Ann Gallagher, Sue Hodge and Nuri Pansari

In the last chapter, you had the opportunity to consider the meaning and elements of consent when people have capacity. As you probably know from your own experience of healthcare, people do not always have capacity to give consent. There are situations when adult patients have fluctuating capacity, when they have severe mental health problems or learning disabilities and when they are unconscious. There are also situations when patients' health problems place them or others at risk and they may be considered as vulnerable adults. In such situations, the health professional has to decide what should be done in that patient's best interests.

This chapter does not examine mental health law in detail but concentrates on situations where the patient lacks capacity to make an autonomous decision. The *Mental Capacity Act 2005* governs the rules in England and Wales. You will find a brief summary of the *Adults with Incapacity (Scotland) Act 2000* at the end of the section 'Capacity, consent and adults' in this chapter (p. 64). At this point it should be mentioned that at the time of writing (May 2011) the Welsh Assembly, having acquired the right to create primary legislation, has passed the *Mental Health (Wales) Measure 2010*. This may mean that, in time, the law will differ in detail between Wales and England. Throughout the United Kingdom, the principles underlying the legislation are similar. The main purpose of the legislation relating to capacity in all parts of the United Kingdom is to ensure that any decision made on behalf of a person who lacks capacity is made for the benefit of that person.

Children and young people present particular challenges for health professionals as their capacity will vary depending on their level of maturity. Generally parents will assume that they have the right to consent on behalf of a child but, as those working with children will be aware, the paramount consideration is the best interests of the child. This does not always coincide with the parents' views. This chapter concentrates on the *Children Act 1989* and Fraser competence.

It is clear that taking consent issues seriously requires a good deal of skill –particularly in communication – and knowledge of the ethical, legal and professional issues.

Two scenarios are presented here that highlight the kind of situations you might encounter in your practice. They will be returned to later in the chapter.

As you read the scenarios please have two questions in mind:

▶ If you were the practitioner, what would you do?
▶ Why would you respond this way? Refer to relevant ethical, legal and professional concepts and arguments that could support your action.

Scenarios

A paramedic's response when compromised capacity threatens the health of another

You are a member of a paramedic crew responding to a call from a woman in the community reporting that she has heard screaming from the house next door. When the crew arrives, accompanied by the police, the door is opened by an elderly woman. She appears distressed and has a bleeding arm wound. She allows the paramedic team to enter but refuses entry to the police. Inside you find a chaotic scene. An elderly man is lying on the floor in the lounge and the glass in the patio door is broken. He has a scalp wound and appears very confused and agitated. The elderly woman is very upset and tells you that her husband has recently been diagnosed with dementia. She tells you that she looks after him but is finding it difficult as he wants to go outside and she fears he will get lost. She tells you that she has to lock the doors so he will not leave and that he had smashed the glass in an attempt to get out. She says that, since his retirement, they have never been separated and do everything together. It is clear that the elderly man, Mr Patel, needs to be taken to hospital but his wife is adamant that this is not what he would want. Mrs Patel asks you to treat him at home and says that she refuses to let him be taken to hospital.

To treat or not to treat: nurse advocacy and a child's refusal

Emily is 14 years old and has end stage renal disease. She has been having dialysis since the age of ten. She had a kidney transplant two years ago, but the organ was rejected after a few months. Emily is on the organ transplant list but no donor has been found so far. Recently her condition has deteriorated and medical staff informed her parents that if she does not receive a kidney transplant soon the outlook is not hopeful. You are a paediatric nurse who has worked with the family for a long time. You have become close to Emily who tells you that she does not want to continue with her dialysis and would prefer to die. She also says that she is afraid to tell her parents.

Capacity, Consent and Adults

You may recall from Chapter 3 that the *Mental Capacity Act 2005* (as amended) states:

> A person must be assumed to have capacity unless it is established that he lacks capacity. s. 1(2)

Lack of capacity is defined as follows:

> a person lacks capacity in relation to a matter if at the material time he is unable to make a decision for himself in relation to the matter because of an impairment of, or a disturbance in the functioning of, the mind or brain. s. 2(1)

The meaning of 'capacity' is more vague. It can mean 'the everyday ability that individuals possess to make decisions or to take actions that influence their life.' In the legal context it is defined as follows:

> capacity refers to a person's ability to do something, including making a decision, which may have legal consequences for the person themselves or for other people. ... [It is] pivotal in balancing the right to autonomy ... and the right to protection from harm. (Letts 2010: 161)

Recognising when Capacity Is Compromised

Whether or not an adult patient lacks capacity to make a decision in relation to a particular issue is a question of fact. A health professional who suspects that there is indeed a lack of capacity must record the facts which have aroused suspicion bearing in mind that the issue is one of capacity to make the decision in question. The level of ability is likely to fluctuate if, for example, the patient has an infection, is under the influence of alcohol, is sedated or in pain.

Assessing Capacity: Who Can Do It and How?

Capacity must be assessed by the health professional who is seeking consent. The issues to be decided by any assessment are set out in

s. 3(1) *Mental Capacity Act 2005*. These are whether or not the patient is able to:

(a) understand the information relevant to the decision,
(b) retain that information,
(c) use or weigh that information as part of the process of making the decision, or
(d) communicate his decision.

Legal aspects

A full analysis of the concept of consent is discussed in Chapter 3 in the context of decision making by a person who has capacity. Once it is established that a patient lacks capacity, then any decision made in relation to that person must be made in his best interests. (*Mental Capacity Act 2005* s. 1(5)). In deciding a patient's best interests, the health professional must take into account and decide what weight to give to all relevant circumstances including the patient's past views and other matters such as the views of family members and the views of other professionals involved with the patient's care. (*Mental Capacity Act 2005* s. 4). It must always be remembered that the health professional remains the person having authority to make the decision and is accountable for the exercise of that authority. The *Mental Capacity Act 2005*: Code of Practice warns 'Anyone who believes that a person lacks capacity should be able to prove their case.' (Code of Practice para. 2.5).

Scotland

The *Adults with Incapacity (Scotland) Act 2000* permits intervention in the affairs of an adult only if:

> the person responsible for authorising or effecting the intervention is satisfied that the intervention will benefit the adult and that such benefit cannot reasonably be achieved without the intervention. (s. 1(2))

The term 'adult' means 'a person who has attained the age of 16 years' (s.1(6)).

An important difference between the Scottish Act and the Act governing England and Wales is the purpose of any intervention – it will 'benefit' the person in Scotland and be in their 'best interests' in England and Wales. Both Acts and relevant Codes of Practice set out similar matters to be taken into account in assessing capacity and in deciding benefit/best interests.

Capacity, Consent and Children

Legal issues relating to consent to medical treatment for children and young adults are more complex and present particular challenges to health professionals. The *Family Law Reform Act 1969* s. 8(1) states that a minor who 'has attained the age of sixteen years' has the same capacity to make healthcare decisions as an adult. It is with the group of children of less than sixteen years that problems can occur. In most cases perhaps, the parents, the health professional and the older child will agree about the child's best interests. This is unfortunately not always the case.

A major change occurred in 1985, following the case of *Gillick v West Norfolk and Wisbech Area Health Authority [1985]* 3 WLR 830 when Victoria Gillick took her local health authority and the Department of Health to court to stop doctors from giving contraceptive advice or treatment to minors of 16 years and under without parental knowledge or consent.

The case eventually went to the House of Lords (now the Supreme Court) which ruled that parental consent was not necessarily required when a young person under the age of 16 sought contraceptive advice. Guidance given by Lord Fraser in that case has established the procedure to be followed in all cases when a person under 16 seeks confidential medical advice. The guidance enables a health professional to decide if the child or young person is 'Fraser competent' (sometimes referred to as 'Gillick competent') and thus able to give or refuse consent.

A health professional needs to establish:

(a) that the child or young person understands the medical issues, that is the nature of the medical condition and the proposed treatment;
(b) the child understands the moral and family issues involved;
(c) that it is in the young patient's best interests that matters should proceed.

In such a situation, the health professional is entitled to rely on the consent or refusal given by the child or young person whether or not the parents have the same views.

Parents do not always accept that in some circumstances their child has the right to exercise autonomy and the right to confidentiality in respect of any treatment without the parents being informed. In 2006, it was confirmed that the principle upheld in *Gillick* did not only apply to issues of contraception but could 'apply to other proposed treatment and advice can be given without parental knowledge' provided the young person fulfils Fraser Guidance. (*R ex p. Sue Axon v Secretary of State for Health and others* [2006] EWHC 37 (Admin) per Silber J at paragraph 87).

Lord Scarman, in *Gillick*, stated that parental rights must 'yield to the child's right to make his own decisions when he reaches sufficient understanding and intelligence to be capable of making up his mind on the matter in question.' Lord Fraser, also in *Gillick*, explained that parental rights 'exist for the benefit of the child and are justified only in so far as they enable a parent to perform his duties towards the child.'

The law may appear relatively straightforward but it can be very complex in practice. Competent minors can consent to treatment but a refusal of treatment deemed to be in the minor's best interests by others, parents or professionals, is sometimes regarded as evidence of the minor's incompetence to make the necessary decision. By way of example Herring (2009) cites

(a) *Re L (Medical Treatment: Gillick competency)* [1998] 2FLR 810 which held that a girl who did not understand the nature of the death that awaited her was incompetent (the facts had not been explained fully to her to avoid causing undue distress);

(b) In the same case the court felt that the girl, who had been brought up as a Jehovah's Witness, had lived a sheltered life because she had not been exposed to a variety of religious views. Her lack of life experience contributed to her lack of competence;

(c) *Re E (A Minor) (Wardship: Medical Treatment)* [1993] 1FLR 386 when the child was held to be incompetent because he did not appreciate the grief his parents would suffer were he to die.

In some cases a young person, who with the support and agreement of parents, refuses life saving medical treatment may find that the decision is overruled by a court if the treatment is considered to be in the child's best interests. In practice, therefore, a child's level of understanding can sometimes be affected by the risk benefit ratio of the proposed treatment.

Capacity and Mental Disorder

In circumstances where capacity is compromised by mental health problems you may need to consider the provisions of the *Mental Health*

Act 1983 (as amended). If a person is suffering 'mental disorder' then the Act permits that person's admission to hospital and detention for:

- assessment (s.2);
- treatment (s.3).

This chapter does not examine the *Mental Health Act 1983* but this is an area you will need to know more about if you work with people who experience mental distress. Further information about the *Mental Health Act* is available at: http://www.dh.gov.uk. A comprehensive exploration of the many ethical issues that arise in mental health practice can be found in Barker (2011).

Ethical aspects

The principle of respect for autonomy is most often cited to justify informed consent in healthcare practice. Patients have a right to make decisions regarding their care and treatment. However, a patient's capacity to make decisions may be compromised by physical or mental ill-health. Edwards (2009: 63–64) distinguished between autonomy and competence. The former he describes as a 'general capacity' of an individual to self-govern and the latter as a more specific capacity to do tasks such as deciding what clothing to wear and how to spend money.

His discussion is helpful in thinking about the ethical aspects of capacity and consent as, for this purpose, you need to consider specific decisions in the healthcare context. The focus of the health professional's attention is not on whether the person is generally autonomous but rather on whether they can weigh up the relevant information in relation to this specific care or treatment decision. When a patient is no longer able to do this, other principles come into play.

You will need to identify the range of interventions that may be appropriate and, in consultation with experienced colleagues, weigh up the benefits (beneficence) and harms or risks (non-maleficence) of each for the patient. The principle of justice is relevant to consent, in situations when capacity is compromised, in a number of ways. First, treating patients fairly involves not discriminating against them on grounds such as age, ethnicity, class, sexual orientation or gender. It should not, for example, be assumed that older and younger patients are less deserving of involvement in decision making or less capable solely on the basis of age. Capacity must always be assumed and every effort made to involve people in decisions about their care and treatment. The four principles provide a helpful framework to think about ethical aspects of the two scenarios (see Chapter 1).

Given the increase in the number of people experiencing dementia, it is helpful to consider a framework that is specifically written to respond to the ethical issues. The Nuffield Council on Bioethics produced such an ethical framework with six components to respond to issues relating to those who experience dementia and their carers. The six components of the ethical framework (Nuffield Council on Bioethics 2009, chapter 2) are as follows:

- *Component 1* – A 'case-based' approach to ethical decisions – there are three stages in this first component: sound moral judgement involves 'identifying and clarifying relevant factual considerations'; 'identifying, interpreting and applying relevant ethical values'; 'comparison with similar situations'.
- *Component 2* – A belief about the nature of dementia – At the time of writing it was estimated that there are approximately 700,000 people in the UK with dementia and it is estimated that this will rise to 1.7 million by 2051. 'Dementia' represents a range of different diseases characterised by progressive deterioration of brain function. Symptoms include memory loss, communication problems, difficulty in managing the activities of everyday life, changes in emotional and psychological responses and physical deterioration. The Nuffield report states that dementia is harmful to the person, that good quality care is important and that people with dementia should not be disadvantaged in the allocation of resources.
- *Component 3* – A belief about quality of life with dementia – two different views about the quality of life of people who experience dementia emerged from the Nuffield consultation exercise before preparing the report. A negative view is that the quality of life with dementia is such that life is not worth living. It was suggested that assisted dying should be legalised and an option. The second view is that good care ensures that the quality of life with those who experience dementia is positive. Some respondents believed that the quality of life with dementia can be as good as for those who do not have dementia. All health and social care professionals can promote the quality of life of those with dementia by responding respectfully and by gaining knowledge and skills in this field of practice.

▶ *Component 4* – The importance of promoting the interests of the person with dementia and those who care for them – three sets of interests are identified in the Nuffield report: those of the person with dementia, those of the carers and those of the professionals. Regarding the person with dementia, the report critiques views of autonomy that focus on rationality, independence and non-interference from others. Additional dimensions of autonomy are suggested: to enable autonomy for a person with dementia requires that they are encouraged to express themselves and this may involve others intervening as advocates to help the person promote autonomy; the second additional aspect of autonomy involves a consideration of how to enhance autonomy. People are not solitary and are rather 'embedded in a network of relationships' (ibid: 27). The point is made that enabling and promoting the autonomy and interests of those with dementia also involves considering the interests of family and friends. This involves offering carers support, information and advice. As traditional views of autonomy focus on rationality, the third addition involves paying attention to and engaging with the person's emotional responses.

The report suggests that well-being of the person with dementia can be promoted by focusing on 'the moment-to-moment experiences (of pleasure and happiness or pain and unhappiness)...even if no memory of that moment's experience is retained' (ibid: 28). An individualised or personalised approach to care is essential here. The interests of carers are considered important because they are deserving of respect as individuals and the role of carer may be challenging. Their relationship with dementia patients is also likely to be enhanced if their interests are considered. Professionals who work with them also have interests and these should not be ignored. Attention needs, therefore, to be paid to their work environment, staffing levels, education and mentoring.

▶ *Component 5* – The requirement to act in accordance with solidarity – the Nuffield report defines solidarity as 'the idea that we are all 'fellow travellers' and that we have duties to support and help each other and in particular those who cannot readily support themselves' (ibid: 29). Solidarity supports the development of research and interventions that destigmatise dementia and that value and assist carers and professionals. There is a close connection between solidarity, as outlined in the report, and justice. It is argued that 'a fair distribution of benefits and burdens should promote and sustain solidarity, realised as a willingness to support persons with dementia throughout the course of their dementia and to help them in maintaining their autonomy as much as possible' (ibid: 30).

▶ *Component 6* – Recognising personhood, identity and value – this final component arises from the implications of philosophical discussion regarding the status of individuals with dementia. There is debate about whether they are a different person or, indeed, a person at all. The latter view is based on ideas of personhood that require a significant level of cognitive functioning that the individual with severe dementia may lack. This view is rejected in the report for two reasons: we do not know what individuals are experiencing – they can still be consider as 'valuers' as they continue to value experiences such as listening to music; and it is limited to view personhood solely in terms of cognition but rather we should consider the emotional and spiritual aspects of the person and their engagement in a network of relationships. Thus it is necessary to broaden the definition of personhood beyond traditional philosophical perspectives.

The Nuffield report refers to the role of dignity in dementia care and suggests that dignity as empowerment is a helpful interpretation. In recent years there has been a wide range of scholarship and research relating to dignity in care. There has also been a number of high profile dignity-promoting initiatives by the Department of Health and professional organisations such as the Royal College of Nursing (RCN). Publications from the RCN (2008) relating to dignity in care and from the Nursing and Midwifery Council (NMC 2010a) relating to the care of older people share common themes of: *people* (staff who are competent, who have positive attitudes and demonstrate helpful behaviours); *process* (emphasises the importance of respectful communication and sensitivity during care activities that render patients vulnerable to indignity); and *place* (attention to the quality of the physical environment and to organisational culture).

The 3 Ps (people, process and place) may be a useful *aide-mémoire* for you as you strive to improve the experiences and promote the interests of patients who both lack and have capacity. These are interpreted a little differently in the RCN and NMC materials but helpfully suggest areas that need to be considered to promote the well-being and dignity of patients. This is particularly important when patients lack capacity and are more dependent on professionals to advance their interests and respond to their needs. A similar framework was discussed by Gallagher (2004) who adds 'policy' as a fourth dimension of dignity in care.

Much of the focus of this discussion has been on ethics as applied to people who experience dementia and older people more broadly; however, the ethical principles and concepts discussed apply equally well to other patient groups. Research relating to the dignity of children and young people, for example, suggest the importance of child and family involvement in decision making and of sensitivity during intimate care procedures (Baillie et al. 2009). Crucially, discussion of the ethical and legal aspects of discussions must focus on the patient's best interests if they lack capacity. (*Mental Capacity Act 2005* s.4).

Professional aspects

The Health Professions Council (HPC) Code does not explicitly refer to advocacy but it seems implied in discussions relating to acting in the best interests of patients. (HPC 2008 para. 1). Advocacy is a means by which individuals can be empowered to express their opinion. As you may recall from Chapter 3, both the Nursing and Midwifery (NMC) and the Health Professions Council (HPC) codes, deal with the issue of consent. Paragraph 9 of the HPC Code (2008) requires health professionals to obtain informed consent to treatment except in cases of emergency. Health professionals are reminded of the competent patient's right to have either consent or refusal fully respected.

Similarly paragraphs 13–17 of the NMC Code (2008 re-published with numbered paragraphs April 2010b) require health professionals to ensure that there is consent to any treatment or care which is delivered, supporting the patient's rights to refuse as well as to consent to treatment.

Advocacy is a role identified in the NMC Code that is particularly important when patient capacity is reduced or lacking. The Code states: You must act as an advocate for those in your care, helping them to access relevant health and social care, information and support' (NMC 2010b Section 4) Advocacy is commonly discussed in relation to nurses and midwives but would seem to be an important component of the role of all health professionals. Fry and Johnstone (2002) discuss three models of advocacy: a rights-protection model (where the professional is a defender of patients' rights); a values-based decision model (where the professional assists patients to discuss their interests, needs and to make choices); and a respect-for-persons model (where the professional focuses on respecting and representing patients' dignity and values particularly when they are unable to do this for themselves). Advocacy as a professional role goes some way toward empowering patients who may lack the capacity, confidence, maturity or language to assert their needs.

Application to Scenarios

A paramedic's response to when compromised capacity threatens the health of another

The scenario is a composite case derived from a number of actual cases. The information suggests that Mr and Mrs Patel have been experiencing difficulties, at least partially, due to Mr Patel's dementia. They are both elderly and appear to be struggling to cope at home. This has resulted in an escalation that led to a paramedic team and the police arriving at their home. In one of the actual cases, the paramedics decided that the elderly gentleman lacked capacity and that it was in his best interests to override his wife's wishes to remain at home. She was initially aggressive but was eventually persuaded to travel to hospital with her husband for a check-up as both had injuries.

Ethical issues

The six components of the Nuffield ethics framework can be helpfully applied to this scenario:

- **Component 1** – A 'case-based' approach to ethical decisions – the identification and clarification of relevant facts in this scenario involves finding out more about the couple's situation: what do we know about their living circumstances? Do they have family and, if so, what is their relationship with them? Should they be contacted for further information with Mrs Patel's consent? Are there specific cultural, religious or language issues that need to be considered? What is their medical history? It would seem helpful to contact the couple's General Practitioner for further information. Is it possible that there is domestic violence in this relationship? The relevant ethical values in this situation could include the four principles of autonomy, beneficence, non-maleficence and justice and also dignity as discussed above.
- **Component 2** – A belief about the nature of dementia – As discussed above, dementia is a growing health problem. It is likely that all health professionals will have contact

with dementia, therefore, there is a strong rationale for them to develop knowledge and skills regarding how to respond therapeutically to people with this diagnosis. Assessing capacity in situations such as this is important. It does not follow that people who have a diagnosis of dementia will lack capacity in relation to all decisions. It appears that Mr Patel may lack capacity as defined by the Mental Capacity Act.

It is therefore the duty of the paramedic to decide what action to take in the patient's best interests. While Mrs Patel's views are important, the paramedic has the responsibility to make, and is accountable for, the decision.

▶ *Component 3* – A belief about quality of life with dementia – it is possible that Mrs Patel is anxious or frightened about the consequences of professional involvement in the life of her husband and herself. She may fear that they will be separated and that the care provided may not meet their needs. She may also fear losing control or perhaps losing their home. It is important, therefore, for the paramedic and other professionals to reassure Mr and Mrs Patel that interventions are intended to improve the quality of their lives. Mrs Patel may be unable to prevent her husband from being hospitalised but it is crucial that health professionals strive to develop a trusting relationship with the couple. Providing information about care options and involving them in care decisions is a prerequisite for quality of care.

▶ *Component 4* – The importance of promoting the interests of persons with dementia and those who care for them – the three sets of interests identified in the Nuffield report are all relevant: Mr Patel has a diagnosis of dementia but we do not know if he is aware of his diagnosis or how he views his situation. He has, we are told, smashed a window suggesting he may feel restrained (see, for example, Hughes 2010). Both he and his wife have injuries but it is not known if these injuries are accidental or non-accidental. It is, therefore, important to consider the interests of Mrs Patel also. Does she feel sufficiently well informed and supported as she cares for her husband? What more could be done to enhance the autonomy of Mr Patel and the well-being of husband and wife. In such situations, health professionals may feel uncomfortable intruding on, what might be considered, a private and potentially humiliating situation for the couple. Health professionals, who encounter such situations, are likely to benefit from clinical supervision and from acquiring dementia care training.

▶ *Component 5* – The requirement to act in accordance with solidarity – the idea that we are 'fellow travellers' and have duties to support and help each other is helpful in responding ethically to Mr and Mrs Patel.

▶ *Component 6* – Recognising personhood, identity and value – this final component reminds us that the focus of attention should be on the individuals who require help. The scenario provides little information about Mr Patel's capacity or health status, therefore, this needs to be investigated. In the first instance, capacity should be assumed and every attempt made to provide him with information and to find out his views and preferences. Time should also be spent with his wife as she is also injured and, therefore, a patient. What follows from the view that both are persons and deserving of respect is that they should be listened to, informed and involved in decisionmaking.

Legal issues

Although it must be presumed that Mr Patel has capacity (*Mental Capacity Act 2005* s.1(2)) the facts would seem to demonstrate that this is not in fact the case. If the paramedic is satisfied that Mr Patel lacks capacity, then it is the paramedic's duty to make the necessary decision in this patient's best interests (*Mental Capacity Act 2005* s.1(5)). While Mrs Patel's views are relevant and must be taken into account, it is the paramedic's duty to make an appropriate decision. (This is discussed in more detail earlier in this chapter.)

Professional issues

Guidance regarding consent in the HPC and NMC codes is applicable to this scenario as capacity must be assumed until it is demonstrated as lacking. Other sections of the code become more pressing when capacity is lacking, for example, protecting and promoting the well-being, health and interests of patients and families.

To treat or not to treat: nurse advocacy and a child's refusal?

In this scenario the nurse is working with a teenager, Emily, with end stage renal disease. The medical staff informed her parents that if she does not receive a kidney transplant soon the outlook is not hopeful. Emily has disclosed to a nurse that she does not want to continue with her dialysis and would prefer to die. The nurse, in this case, suggested to Emily that she should talk with her parents and offered to be present if this would be helpful.

Emily did talk with her parents and during an emotional discussion she told them how she felt. Emily's parents said they had no idea she felt like this and had assumed that, like them, she wanted every possible piece of information that would help her to survive. With the nurse's help, they were able to listen to each other and to agree that stopping treatment should be considered. It was agreed that a meeting with the professionals involved would be arranged. During the meeting the treatment and care options for Emily were explained and discussed. The family's decision was to discontinue treatment and palliative care options were explored. The consensus was that Emily should have as good a quality of life as possible in the time she had left.

A young person who has the capacity to consent to straightforward, relatively risk-free treatment may not necessarily have the capacity to consent to complex treatment involving high risks or serious consequences. In Emily's situation her parents were not aware of her wishes. At fourteen years of age, Emily may be competent in accordance with the Fraser Guidance to give or refuse her own consent. It could be argued that her past history means that she has good insight into her situation. However, Emily had not told you that she does not want her parents to know that she no longer wants treatment. It would appear therefore that she needed support to help her share this information with her parents. As a health professional your primary duty is towards the patient. Emily may have been frightened of the response of her parents to her wishes. The role of the nurse as patient advocate here is to help her to share her wishes with her parents and not to be seen as being biased towards either Emily or her parents' views.

Ethical issues

It seems likely that an intelligent 14 year old with a long-term condition will be sufficiently autonomous to understand and weigh up information regarding treatment. This should not be assumed and her capacity to make such a significant decision should be assessed. As it happened, the parents in this case agreed with the teenager's decision and there was no conflict. If they had disagreed with her decision this would have been a much more challenging situation. It seems possible that the professionals in this scenario may have come to different conclusions weighing benefits (beneficence) and harms (non-maleficent) differently. Those who were in favour of continued treatment may have argued in terms of the prolongation of life and the possibility of a successful future transplant or other treatment. Those arguing against treatment may have cited quality of life arguments with a view to sparing further suffering and enabling the young person to live well until she died. Happily, both she and her parents agreed that treatment could be discontinued and they could plan together how they should spend the remainder of their precious time together. Regarding the principle of justice, the issue of the shortage of organs is a very real challenge and many patients remain on the waiting list.

Legal issues

Another aspect of justice in this scenario suggests the importance of approaching the capacity of children and young people in a fair and measured way. It might, for example, be suggested that expectations of children regarding consent are more onerous than those required of adults. In *Re MB [1997] Med LR 217,* for example, Lord Scarman stated that it is necessary to ask whether the child 'has sufficient discretion to enable him or her to make a wise choice in his or her own interest'.

Emily has not in fact refused treatment. Had she done so then the question of her competence to decide would arise. It may be that she has such competence but remember the difficulties illustrated by the case law discussed previously which may be faced by a child who disagrees with parents and/or health professionals.

Professional issues

The guidance in the HPC and NMC codes relating to consent are also applicable here. These need to be considered in the context of law relating to children and young people. In any case, it is important that the health professional takes seriously the role of patient advocate so that the well-being, preferences and interests of the young person are central to the discussion.

Conclusion

This chapter has explored some of the many issues relating to consent when capacity may be compromised by illness, disability or age. The scenarios suggest that caution should be exercised when assessing capacity. It should not be assumed that an adult with dementia or a young person lacks capacity and is, therefore, unable to make decisions, nor should it be assumed that they have capacity. A careful and fair assessment of capacity is necessary. It is also important to consider the patient in the context of their families and relationships where possible, and to respond sensitively and respectfully assuming and striving towards solidarity.

Jones (in Watts 2009: 22) puts it this way:

> The respect we should have for non-autonomous persons, then, is not rooted in an abstract judgement of which beings possess a rational nature and can thus be 'deduced' to deserve respect. Our respect for the other is rooted rather in an immediate recognition of a fellow member of our community, or one who could and should be a member if we show the proper solidarity that it is in our nature to show.

Acknowledgement

The authors would like to thank Verity Snook for her help with a scenario for this chapter.

References

Baillie, L., Ford, P., Gallagher, A. & Wainwright, P. (2009) Dignified care for children and young people: nurses' perspective. *Paediatric Nursing*, 21(2), 24–28.

Barker, P. (Ed.) (2011) *Mental Health Ethics: The Human Context*. Routledge, London.

Department of Health, *Mental health Act*, http://www.dh.gov.uk/en/ Publicationsandstatistics/Legislation/Actsandbills/DH_4002034 Accessed 23 January 2011.

Edwards, S. (2009) *Nursing Ethics: A Principle-Based Approach* (2nd ed.). Palgrave Macmillan, Basingstoke.

Fry, S. & Johnstone, M-J. (2002) *Ethics in Nursing Practice: A Guide to Ethical Decision Making*. Blackwell Publishing, Oxford.

Gallagher, A. (2004) 'Dignity and respect for dignity – two key health professional values: implications for everyday nursing practice' in *Nursing Ethics* 11(6), 587–599.

Health Professions Council (2008) *Standards of Conduct, Performance and Ethics. HP*C, London.

Herring, J. (2009) *Family Law* (4th ed.). Longman Harlow, Essex, pp. 453– 454.

Hughes, E. (Ed.) (2010) *Rights, Risks and Restraint-Free Care of Older People.* Jessica Kingsley Publishers, London.

Jones, D.A. (2009) 'Incapacity and personhood: respecting the non-autonomous self' in Watts, H. (Ed.) *Incapacity and Care: Controversies in Healthcare and Research.* The Linacre Centre, Oxford.

Letts, P. (General Editor) (2010) *Assessment of Mental Capacity – A Practical Guide for Doctors and Lawyers* (3rd ed.). British Medical Association and the Law Society, London.

Mental Capacity Act Code of Practice. TSO, London.

Nuffield Council on Bioethics (2009) *Dementia: Ethical Issues.* Nuffield Council on Bioethics, London.

Nursing and Midwifery Council (2010a) *Guidance for the Care of Older People.* NMC, London.

Nursing and Midwifery Council (2010b) *The Code: Standards of Conduct, Performance and Ethics for Nurses and Midwives.* NMC, London.

Royal College of Nursing (2008) *Defending Dignity: Challenges and Opportunities for Nursing.* RCN, London.

Chapter 5
Truth telling

Anne Arber and Caroline Wade

There are many questions to consider when thinking about truth telling in the healthcare context: should you tell patients the truth, the whole truth and nothing but the truth? How should you respond when the truth is unknown or uncertain, for example, when a diagnosis cannot be confirmed? What ethical and professional principles offer guidance in relation to truth telling? What skills do you need to share unwelcome information with patients and families?

In healthcare practice, there are shared professional values relating to honesty, openness and integrity and these values are represented in codes of conduct. It is therefore difficult to justify withholding information or deceiving patients regarding, for example, their diagnosis or prognosis. Lying to patients, in particular, undermines trust between patient and professional. Our objectives for this chapter are to critically examine the role of health professionals in relation to truth telling; to discuss paternalistic and shared models of decision making; to discuss the ethical, legal and professional issues that arise in relation to truth telling.

We begin, as in other chapters, with two scenarios related to truth telling. As you read the scenarios please have two questions in mind:

- If you were the professional, what would you do?
- Why would you respond this way? Refer to relevant ethical, legal and professional concepts and arguments that could support your action

Scenarios

Should the paramedic tell the truth?

A paramedic team receives an emergency call to assist Mr George Stein, a 65 year old man with acute onset of headache, slurred speech and reduced movement in his right arm and leg. You are a paramedic called to deal with the situation. You quickly recognise that Mr Stein is presenting with the symptoms of a stroke and you arrange for his transfer to the local hospital. Mr Stein is anxious about being taken to hospital. You are settling Mr Stein down in the ambulance and when checking his vital signs he asks you a direct question: 'Am I having a stroke?'

When bad news has not been received: nurse responses

You are a nurse on the night shift in an Intensive care Unit (ICU). During the handover report you are told that Mrs Franchi, a seriously ill patient, has suddenly died. You are told that all the close family and next of kin had been informed of her death and have been to view the body. Mrs Franchi is still in the ICU and last offices are about to be carried out. Fifteen minutes into the night shift the daughter of the deceased, Isabella, arrived at the ICU in a very distressed state, crying hysterically. You have not met Isabella before. You greet the daughter sympathetically. Isabella is very hurried and agitated and pushes past you into the intensive care unit saying 'I want to see my mother'. She makes her way to her mother's room and you follow. She opens the door of her mother's room and says in a shocked and distressed voice: 'but she looks dead, nurse?'

Being Truthful: Patient's Best Interests?

Telling the truth has been shown to increase patient compliance, reduce morbidity associated with medical interventions and improve health outcomes and relationships (Turkoski 2001). However, not all patients want truthfulness about their health (Tuckett 2004) and patients are known to suffer distress when disclosure is handled insensitively such as in breaking bad news (Costello 2010). As a professional you are likely to agree that telling lies and half truths are morally discredited healthcare practices and are unethical.

Telling patients the truth about their diagnoses is, however, a fairly recent phenomenon in healthcare practice. Historically, patients were dependent on a physician's professional knowledge and authority. Many people believed that the doctor knew best and that the medical profession would act in such a way as to serve their best interests. Acting to maintain the best interests of patients may in the past have resulted in doctors withholding bad news from patients for fear of causing further distress. Some professionals may, for example, avoid giving a terminal prognosis for fear of the effect it may have. Professionals acting in the best interests of patients may result in patients being seen as passive recipients of treatment and medical care.

Acting in the patient's best interests can result in a paternalistic approach. Paternalism is defined as government or rule by a father and implies that a father will act in the best interests of his children and will sometimes make decisions for them. In healthcare the idea is that a professional who has advanced training and skills is well placed to make decisions for patients (Beauchamp & Childress 2009). Two types of paternalism are discussed in the literature: soft paternalism and hard paternalism. Soft paternalism involves 'an agent interven[ing] in the life of another person on grounds of beneficence or non-maleficence with the goal of preventing substantially *nonvoluntary conduct'* (Beauchamp & Childress 2009: 209).

Examples of non-voluntary conduct might include situations where a patient's autonomy is compromised by illness so is unable to make a fully informed choice. The intention is to try 'to prevent the harmful consequences of a patient's actions that the patient did not autonomously choose' (ibid: 210). Hard paternalism, on the other hand, 'involves interventions intended to prevent or mitigate harm to or to benefit a person, despite the fact that the person's risky choices and actions are informed, voluntary and autonomous' (ibid: 210). The hard paternalist will then justify overriding the patient's autonomy by restricting the information or by overriding the person's autonomous choices. The soft paternalist will manage information and take decisions for patients considered to lack substantial autonomy. Deciding who is substantially autonomous or non-autonomous and which actions are harmful or beneficial is a matter of professional judgement and there may be disagreement. You may remember Lord Steyn's comment that 'In modern law medical paternalism no longer rules' (*Chester v Ashfar* [2004] UKHL 41 at para. 16 – see Chapter 3, p. 46).

Ethical aspects

Truth telling in healthcare is supported by the principles of autonomy, beneficence, non-maleficence and justice. It is also based on veracity, a concept which is defined as the 'comprehensive, accurate, and objective transmission of information, as well as to the way the professional fosters the patient's [...] understanding' (Beauchamp & Childress 2009: 289). The emphasis in this definition is on helping the patient to understand healthcare information. This is a process which results in the communication of accurate and comprehensive information. Veracity is also an obligation based on respect developed in our relationships with patients. Patients have a right to truthful disclosures, which depend on relationships of trust. You may, however, find yourself in situations where medical information is withheld from patients perhaps due to pressure from families. In such situations, non-disclosure, limited disclosure, deception or lying may be considered when veracity and the principle of autonomy is thought to conflict with other ethical obligations (Beauchamp & Childress 2009).

Patient autonomy is an important ethical principle in relation to truth telling and the right to information. The principle of respecting the autonomy of the patient 'includes building or maintaining others' capacities for autonomous choice while helping to allay fears and other conditions that destroy or disrupt autonomous action' (Beauchamp & Childress 2009: 103). In this view, patients have a right to information that enables them to act autonomously. However, it is important also to identify the role of the health professional in identifying patients' wishes and promoting autonomy. This includes finding out what patients wish regarding the receipt of information that can help them to make decisions (Beauchamp & Childress 2009). The other three principles – beneficence, non-maleficence and justice – can and should also be brought to bear in relation to truth telling. Is it, for example, the case that the benefits outweigh the harm? Is it just to withhold information from some patients (for example, older patients, children or those with learning disabilities) and not from others?

In contemporary healthcare a paternalistic approach, particularly hard paternalism, is challenged. Advances in medicine and communication literacy such as information technology, use of the world wide web, and the emergence of patient support groups towards the latter part of the 20th century, have helped patients to become more questioning and knowledgeable about their healthcare. Patient empowerment is supported by policy directives, for example, the 'expert patient' programme (Department Health 2001) and user involvement in health-care (Beresford et al. 2007). The policy and practice environment rec-ognises that patients can become 'expert' about their own condition, services and treatment. The recent £12 million awareness campaign launched by the Department of Health (DH) to help people remember the first signs of stroke and help the public understand when a stoke was happening (DH 2009) demonstrates the commitment of the DH to increasing the knowledge and awareness of the public. This is a three year campaign to promote public awareness as part of the National Stroke Strategy.

In the 21st century more egalitarian relationships are developing between health professionals and patients. Patients are demanding more say in their care and treatment and a new model of shared decision making has emerged (Lupton 2003). The shared decision-making model acknowledges the right of patients to hold and express their own values and beliefs, to make informed choices by being able to weigh the risks and benefits of treatments available to them and take actions that best promote their health and well-being (Glass & Cluxton 2004). The shared decision-making model is based on a patient's right to the truth and the establishment and preservation of trust between patient and HPC. Trust forms the basis of the health professional–patient relationships and effectively sharing knowl-edge and information with patients in a collaborative model of care is prioritised.

The relationship between the patient and the professional is the bed-rock of healthcare practice. Relationships of trust are very important to the whole of healthcare practice. Mistrust will compromise the thera-peutic relationship between the health professional and the patient (Tuckett 2004). You may have had experience of situations where trust has broken down and where professionals have to pick up the pieces and where complaints about care and treatment are received.

As health professionals take on new roles they are increasingly responsible and accountable when informing patients about their condition and response to treatment. In the past giving a diagnosis and further information was the prerogative of doctors but this has now changed as new roles have developed and there are new working arrangements involving team work and advanced practice roles with nurses and allied health professionals having extended practice roles and responsibilities for information giving.

Legal aspects

From a legal point of view, there is no specific legal right to be given information relating to health issues. BUT it must be remembered that in order to give a valid consent a patient must be given adequate and accurate information. (See Chapter 3 at p. 46.) Indirectly there might be a right to information if it is remembered that failure to give appropriate information may mean that any consent to treatment is negated. This could give rise to an action for negligence or trespass to the person. (See Chapter 3 at p. 50.)

The legal requirement to give accurate information to enable a patient to exercise an autonomous choice was discussed in Chapter 3. It seems to be assumed that any information given to the patient will be truthful.

Generally a legal duty to tell the truth will only be enforced if a false statement is made under oath or with dishonest intent to obtain some benefit. In the context of healthcare practice it is, however, possible that a duty will be indirectly enforced. It has already been seen that consent can be negated if it has been obtained on the basis of untruths (the tort of trespass to the person). Failure to give full accurate information enabling a person to exercise autonomy may amount to the tort of negligence. The law relating to information giving is complex. The rules effectively mean that a person is entitled to be given full and true information on which to base a decision. Persons who are able to establish that consent would not have been given had they been made aware of all the facts may be able to bring a successful claim for damages for negligence.

While there is no doubt that a patient is entitled to be given enough information to enable an autonomous decision to be made, there may be occasions when the health professional believes that certain information needs to be withheld in the patient's best interest. This is sometimes referred to as *'therapeutic privilege'*. When information has been withheld, the patient may allege that consent would not have been given had the full truth been explained. In such a case '... there is the need that the doctor should have the opportunity of proving that he reasonably believed that disclosure of the risk would be damaging to his patient or contrary to his best interest.' (per Lord Scarman in *Sidaway v Bethlem RHG* [1985] 1 All ER 643.).

Truth telling is difficult in some cases. Were the duty to tell the truth to be regarded as absolute, the risk of causing actual psychological injury might arise. Initially such injury was only actionable when the person suffering injury was the direct victim. In recent years the courts have recognised that in some cases a person, who is not the direct victim, may succeed in an action for negligence when such injury is caused by the impact of the injuries sustained by the direct victim. This rather difficult concept is demonstrated by the following case.

McLoughlin v O'Brian [1983] 1 ACX 410

Mrs M's husband and three children were involved in a traffic accident. On reaching the hospital about an hour later, Mrs M found that one child was dead. The other two children were seriously injured. Both children and her husband were in shock and were yet to be cleaned up and made comfortable. As a result, Mrs M suffered identifiable psychiatric injury. In holding that there could be liability for purely psychological injury sustained by an indirect (secondary) victim, Lord Bridge said

I can see no grounds whatever for suggesting that to make the defendant liable for reasonably foreseeable psychiatric illness caused by his negligence would be to impose a crushing burden on him out of proportion to his moral responsibility.

Professional aspects

Codes of professional conduct provide guidance regarding the disclosure of information. The Health Professions Council (HPC) Standards (HPC 2008) by emphasising the best interests of patients (Section 1), confidentiality (Section 2), maintaining proper and effective communication (Section 7) and integrity and honesty (Section 14). The Nursing and Midwifery Council's Standards (NMC 2008a) also prescribes respect for people's right to confidentiality (Sections 5–7), sharing information in a form that people understand (Sections 11–12) and respecting people's right to accept or refuse treatment and care. This could include refusing information. In discussing honesty and integrity, the NMC Code also requires that professionals must 'give a constructive and honest response to anyone who complains about the care they have received' (Section 52).

In these codes of conduct there is support for patient autonomy and the right to information but also the acknowledgement that patients have a right to refuse information. Skill in eliciting the patients' readiness for information and their wishes in relation to being involved in decision making is important (Arber & Gallagher 2003). Arguments to support the withholding of negative information are commonly justified on the basis of beneficence (doing good), where for example too much information at an inappropriate time could lead to traumatic shock. Failure to give full information or giving information in a way that is misleading could lead to legal action and claims of negligence. Informed consent is, for example, not possible if the patient is not adequately informed.

Application to Scenarios

Truth telling may raise ethical dilemmas for health professionals. The principles and interpretation of the truth may vary across clinical contexts, cultures and roles. The two scenarios raise key issues in truth telling and both scenarios are based on real life situations.

Should the paramedic tell the truth?

The first scenario highlights a dilemma for a professional, Adam, in the context of diagnostic uncertainty. In the real situation, the paramedic was surprised by the patient's question 'am I having a stroke?' He replied: 'I don't know. You will need to be seen by a doctor at the hospital who will answer your questions'.

What do you think about this answer? How would you have responded? The paramedic is uncertain about Mr Stein's diagnosis until further tests have been carried out. However, he is conversant with the signs of a stoke and thinks that it is quite likely that Mr Stein has had a stroke. The paramedic may have been uncomfortable with his answer as he may have felt he was avoiding the question asked. Mr Stein would like an answer to the question. He may have some understanding of the signs of a stroke from the recent TV advertising campaign or perhaps from personal experience. The evasive answer by the paramedic may have made him feel more anxious or frustrated. This scenario highlights how a professional feels unable to tell the truth because of diagnostic uncertainty and is, perhaps, experiencing some difficulty in handling a challenging question.

So what are the ethical and professional issues related to this scenario?

Taking care of the patient and avoiding harm to the patient

In the actual situation there was evidence that Adam, the paramedic, demonstrated appropriate skills in identifying and assessing Mr Stein's health and social care needs (HPC 2008). He considered the best interests of the patient and his scope of practice. However, he needed to weigh up the benefits and potential harm to the patient of confirming a diagnosis in the context of medical uncertainty. A diagnosis of stroke requires neurological examination and scans and is primarily a medical responsibility. Mr Stein is clearly anxious and distressed and Adam wishes to avoid causing further harm to the patient. He may lack the essential communication skills to address this patient's question. His 'I don't know' may be considered a partially truthful (that is, 'I don't know for sure') response as Adam has insufficient medical evidence to confirm a diagnosis.

Avoidance strategy

It might be claimed that Adam is using an avoidance strategy by responding as he does to Mr Stein's question. If he told the truth and gave Mr Stein the 'significant news' that he may be having a stroke he may have caused further distress to the patient both physical and emotional. Giving such news may cause adverse physiological effects. For example, there could be a rise in blood pressure, pulse rate and respiratory rate in response to stress and increased oxygen demand (Marieb 2006), which could have exacerbated Mr Stein's condition. These worries are understandable and well founded. However, this is a patient who is asking for information directly.

Adam, the paramedic, may believe he is acting in the best interests of his patient in terms of beneficence and non-maleficence but he has compromised Mr Stein's ability to be an autonomous participant in his own healthcare by not addressing his question fully. You may find that definitions of 'best interests' vary among professionals, patients and family members. In a legal context, 'best interests' is explained in different ways by different statutes, for example, the *Mental Capacity Act 2005* s.4 and the *Children Act 1989* s.1(1). In very general terms, a patient's 'best interests' must be determined by taking into account all relevant facts including the specific circumstances of the specific person in the specific situation.

As discussed above, professional codes emphasise the need for professionals to be truthful. However, medical uncertainty complicates the issues as professionals do not always have full information to support the accurate communication of information. In modern health care practice, however, professionals have a role to provide accurate information. Many would argue that giving accurate information and significant news requires specialist training in advanced communication skills (Wilkinson et al. 2003). Without training in handling difficult questions and giving significant news, professionals may use distancing strategies that block communication such as referring patients (you may have heard this referred to a 'passing the buck') to other health professionals or strategies of avoidance.

Steps in giving significant news

Mr Stein asked a direct question suggesting his knowledge and understanding of his predicament. Therefore Mr Stein is to some degree prepared for the news that he may be having a stroke. It is recommended that HCPs develop good knowledge of the patient, their wishes and build a relationship based on rapport and trust. In the situation we describe there is a lack of congruence between what the patient wishes to know, his needs and the response of the professional (Salander 2002). Mr Stein did feel comfortable to ask for information about his health. Adam did not use a strategy to take this question that would enable him to assess the patient's knowledge and to answer the question in a supportive and honest manner that would not cause harm to the patient.

How would you go about taking this question? One way to respond to Mr Stein's question is to gather further information, for example, he could ask 'what makes you think you're having a stroke?' This would provide further information about Mr Stein's knowledge of his condition. For example, it is possible that Mr Stein may have had a stroke in the past as well as being aware of the recent publicity about the signs and symptoms of a stroke (DH 2009). Rudnick (2002) acknowledges that health professionals have different skills and approaches when delivering significant news and the setting in which the news is delivered is important. All authors acknowledge that the emotional aspects of giving and receiving significant news should be tailor made to specific situations.

The paramedic may believe that he was protecting his patient from harm by not answering his question and referring it to the doctor. His omission to establish and respect his patient's wishes could result in compromising the principles of patient autonomy, informed consent and respect for human rights. Had he asked Mr Stein why he thought he might be having a stroke, he would have been able to establish how well informed he was about his condition. This would form a basis to invite Mr Stein into further discussion, providing the opportunity for both parties to be fully involved in establishing his patient's wishes, needs and readiness for information about his condition (NHS Centre for Reviews and Dissemination 2000). Trustworthiness can be demonstrated by using a warm and caring tone, demonstrating kindness, considerateness and empathy, which play an important role in the process of communication and truth telling (Ptacek & Ptacek 2001; Salander 2002), and this approach facilitates the delivery of the truth in a sensitive and concise manner (Glass & Cluxton 2004). Fobbing the patient off to another professional may not be received as effective communication by the patient and may affect the relationship of trust. Assessing a patient's readiness to receive significant news is an important skill for professionals.

Glass and Cluxton (2004) highlight that in general health professionals are trusted and respected for their honesty. The Nursing Midwifery Council (2008) and the Health Professions Council (2008) both highlight the importance of being open and honest. The respective codes of conduct also say that it is important not to damage the public's confidence in the profession. In some situations, such as this one, the most ethical response uses effective communication skills to determine what is behind the patient's question, to admit uncertainty where this is truthful and to point out that further investigations are required to confirm or challenge a likely diagnosis. The paramedic could have asked Mr Stein, as suggested above 'why do you ask?' and then if he demonstrated that he suspected a stroke it could be followed up with 'I can't be sure as you would need to have further investigations. But it is possible.'

When bad news has not been received: nurse responses

In relation to scenario 2 how would you have reacted in this situation? In the actual case the night nurse, Jane, is taken by surprise as she has been told by the nurses on the day shift that all the close relatives and next of kin have been informed that Mrs Franchi has died. We now examine the ethical, legal and professional issues that arise in relation to each scenario.

It is not difficult to see how the nurse got into difficulties when the patient's daughter turned up unexpectedly in ICU, expecting to see her mother alive. The nurse is working with the assumption that the patient's daughter knows that her mother is dead. This is confirmed to her by the degree of distress exhibited by the patient's daughter when she arrives at the ICU. Importantly the daughter has never seen a dead body before and she has come to the hospital on her own and it is late at night. What would you do should a situation like this occur?

What are the ethical and professional issues related to this scenario?

Taking care of the relative and avoiding harm

Mrs Franchi's daughter Isabella is distressed and agitated as her mother is dangerously ill in the ICU. She is aware that her mother could die at any time. She arrives on the ICU alone expecting to see her mother still alive. However, during her journey from home to hospital her mother has died. Isabella was desperate to get to her mother's bedside before she died. She has never seen a dead body before and she is on her own and very distressed and anxious.

Jane is in charge of the ICU when Isabella arrives there. She is being very kind to Isabella and welcomes her warmly but she has been led to believe that all Mrs Franchi's family know of their mother's death so she is completely unprepared for Isabella turning up and assumes she knows what has happened. Instead of taking control of the situation and slowing down what was happening Jane lets Isabella proceed to her mother's room where to Isabella's horror and distress she finds her mother dead. Jane feels mortified by what has happened. There are many ways this scenario could have been avoided.

Avoiding assumptions

Clearly Isabella has no knowledge of what has happened but the assumption has been made by members of the nursing team that all family members know of their mother's death. It is very important to avoid making assumptions about what people know. It is important that Jane should clarify and assess Isabella's understanding of her mother's situation in a private place and in a sensitive way. This allows for privacy and dignity of the relative and supports Isabella's human rights. This also supports the ethical principles of beneficence and non- maleficence.

Slowing down the pace of the interaction

Isabella is very anxious and worried about her desperately ill mother. She therefore is very rushed when she enters the ICU and dashes to her mother's side. In this situation it is important for Jane to try to slow Isabella down. This can be done by taking Isabella to a private area away from interruptions and being seated in a comfortable space, which demonstrates respect for Isabella's dignity (Ptacek & Ptacek 2001; Kaye 1996). She could then find out what Isabella knows of her mother's situation using sensitive communication skills. For example, using an empathetic approach Jane could say: 'I can see you are very distressed, Isabella' and wait for Isabella's reply. Jane could also start by asking an open ended question to assess Isabella's understanding: 'Can you tell me what you understand about your mother's condition?' Jane could also find out if Isabella may want to have another family member with her. Most people like to receive significant and bad news by having another family member or friend with them.

Use of a warning shot

Most experts in breaking bad news highlight the importance of giving a 'warning shot' so that the relative can prepare for the terrible news that her mother has died (Buckman 1992; Fallowfield & Jenkins 2004). Kaye (1996) discusses preparation for giving bad news and preparing the patient/relative by giving a verbal warning shot that bad news is about to be given. By taking Isabella to a private area and then asking about her knowledge of her mother's condition a nurse can prepare the daughter psychologically for receiving the news of her mother's death. This approach also gives the health professional(s) a little time to prepare to break the news to Isabella. Unfortunately Jane was feeling rushed and felt unprepared to give Isabella a warning shot about her mother's death. Both Jane and Isabella were shocked and distressed by each other's reaction.

Emotional labour

Truth telling and breaking significant news involves a degree of emotional labour by the health professional(s). Emotional labour has been defined as: 'the labour involved in dealing with other peoples' feelings' (James 1989). Professionals, for example, have to manage their own emotions in the breaking of bad news and patients have to deal with the emotional implications of receiving it. Dunnice and Slevin (2000) found that nurses described how they experienced distress, such as helplessness and anger, during bad news disclosures by 'being there' with the patient. It is important that health professional(s) have good support and clinical supervision to support them in giving significant news. Jane was devastated and mortified about how she broke the news to

Isabella and she justifiably felt very angry with her team in relation to the inaccurate information she received. Jane was determined to reflect and learn from this situation so she developed some practical strategies for use in the future to handle a similar situation. She said how important it is to avoid working with assumptions and the importance of giving a warning shot to the relative when bad news is going to be broken. She also met the team to discuss her experience and reflect on good practice in relation to truth telling and breaking significant news. Professionally and morally Jane wants to be a 'good nurse' and effective at managing her own and others' emotions. She is caring but feels she let herself and the patient's daughter down on this occasion.

Conclusion

Truth telling and breaking bad news are significant aspects of the roles of health professionals. Telling the truth is embedded in the professional codes of practice of all health professionals; and rightly so as the public wish to be treated with respect and truth telling is a fundamental principle in building trust and rapport with people. Truth telling in clinical practice with patients is not unlike our perspective on truth telling in social life in that it is considered a virtue and an obligation as well as a duty and in this sense it is a universal law (Tuckett 2004). In practice it is sometimes difficult and confusing for us when working with anxious and worried patients and relatives as we want to do our best for the people we care for and not to cause further distress. While most patients and families want to know the truth about the illness, there are instances when withholding the truth is permissible. For example, if a patient asks not to be given information, withholding the truth can be justified by taking into account the patient's own wishes. This approach still supports patient autonomy. Forcing the truth on an unwilling patient could be detrimental to well-being (Beauchamp & Childress 2009). There is also a legal and professional impetus to disclose information to patients. Decisions to waive information may pose challenges to professionals particularly related to gaining informed consent. Both the NMC and HPC professional codes of practice also support the sharing of information.

Truth telling in practice can be difficult due to concerns that any significant news could be harmful. For some patients hope relies on the possible rather than the probable outcomes and disclosing the truth may destroy any hope the patient has, which results in despair

(Ruddick 1999). The fostering of hope has been shown to have a therapeutic effect on health, particularly for patients with cancer (Rustoen & Handstead 1998). Telling the truth and breaking bad news where patients and relatives still feel supported also require that health professional(s) have good communication skills. Using good communication skills means that the ethical principles of veracity, autonomy and beneficence can be supported. It is always important to assess readiness for information; to feel able to respond appropriately to direct questions and avoiding blocking behaviours which close communication down and challenge trust. It is very important the health professional(s) do not work with assumptions about patient preferences and that preferences are always elicited from patients. To not elicit preferences suggests a paternalistic approach and health professional(s) need to consider if this is soft or hard paternalism and when, if ever, this is justifiable. Cultural values and beliefs have been shown to influence truth telling. There may be cultural rules and taboos related to disclosure. It is therefore always necessary to be sensitive to cultural requirements around the disclosure of information and truth telling.

References

Arber, A. and Gallagher, A. (2003) Breaking bad news revisited: the push for negotiated disclosure and changing practice implications. *International Journal of Palliative Nursing*, 9(4) 166–172.

Beauchamp, T.L. & Childress, J.F. (2009) *Principles of Biomedical Ethics* (6th ed.). Oxford, Oxford University Press.

Beresford, P., Adshead, C. & Croft, S. (2007) *Palliative Care, Social Work and Service Users. Making Life Possible.* Jessica Kingsley, London.

Buckman, R. (1992) *How to Break Bad News.* London Papermac.

Costello, J. (2010) Truth telling and the palliative diagnosis. *International Journal of Palliative Nursing*, 16(1), 3.

Department of Health (2001) *The Expert Patient: A New Approach to Chronic Disease Management for the 21st Century.* London, Department of Health.

Department of Health (2009) Department of Health announces new stroke advertising initiative http://www.stroke.org.uk/media_centre/news/department_of_health.html [Accessed 2 June 2010].

Dunnice, U. & Slevin, E. (2000) Nurses' experiences of being present with a patient receiving a diagnosis of cancer. *Journal of Advanced Nursing* 32(3), 611–618.

Fallowfield, L. & Jenkins, V. (2004) Communicating sad, bad and difficult news in medicine. *The Lancet*, 363, 312–19.

Glass, E. & Cluxton, D. (2004) Truth Telling: Ethical issues in clinical practice. *Journal of Hospice and Palliative Nursing,* 6(4), 232–242.

Health Professions Council (2008) Standards of Conduct, performance and ethics. HPC London.

James, N. (1989) Emotional labour: skill and work in the social regulation of feelings. *Sociological Review.* 37(1), 15–42.

Kaye, P. (1996) *Breaking Bad News A 10 Step Approach*. EPL Publications Northampton.

Lupton, D. (2003). *Medicine as Culture*. London, Sage publications.

Marieb, E. (2006) *Essentials of Human Anatomy and Physiology* (8th ed.). Pearson Education, San Francisco.

NHS Centre for Reviews and Dissemination (2000) *Effective Health Care: Informing, Communicating and Sharing Decisions with People Who Have Cancer.* The University of York.

Nursing Midwifery Council (2008) *The Code*: *Standards of Conduct, Performance and Ethics.* NMC London.

Ptacek, J.T. & Ptacek, J.J. (2001) Patients' Perceptions of Receiving Bad News about Cancer. *Journal of Clinical Oncology,* 19(21), 4160–4164.

Ruddick, W. (1999) Hope and deception. *Bioethics,* 13(3–4), 343–357.

Rudnick, A (2002) Informed Consent to Breaking Bad News. *Nursing Ethics*, 61–66

Rustoen, T. & Hanstead, B.R. (1998) Nursing intervention to increase hope in cancer patients. *Journal of Clinical Nursing,* 7, 19–27.

Salander, P. (2002) Bad news from the patient perspective: an analysis of the written narratives of newly diagnosed cancer patients. *Social Science and Medicine,* 55(5), 721–732.

Tuckett, A.G. (2004) Truth-telling in clinical practice and the arguments for and against: a review of the literature. *Nursing Ethics,* 11(5), 500–513.

Turkoski, B.B. (2001) Ethics in the absence of truth. *Home Healthcare Nurse*. 19(4), 218–222.

Wilkinson, S.M., Leliopoulou, C., Gambles, M. & Roberts, A. (2003) Can intensive three day programmes improve nurses' communication skills in cancer care? *Psycho-Oncology,* 12, 1–13.

Chapter 6
Confidentiality

Pat Colliety and Khim Horton

As a health professional you have access to a wide range of personal information about patients. You are trusted to keep this information private and to use it only for the purposes for which it was given. There are circumstances when you will know it is not acceptable to share patient information and other circumstances when it is not only acceptable but required. You need also to be aware that there are exceptional situations when you may have to share confidential information without the patient's consent.

This chapter examines the concept of confidentiality clarifying what it means and why it matters. We have chosen to illustrate this with two scenarios related to particularly vulnerable groups, young people and older people. We consider the legal, ethical and professional aspects of confidentiality to help prepare you to manage patient information appropriately. The healthcare scenarios selected demonstrate different aspects of confidentiality. They illustrate that confidentiality is not so straightforward and requires critical analysis and an understanding of ethical and legal principles and professional codes.

As you read the scenarios please have two questions in mind:

- If you were the professional, what would you do?
- Why would you respond this way? Refer to relevant ethical, legal and professional concepts and arguments that could support your action.

Scenarios

'Don't tell my parents': a nurse's dilemma

Constance is 14 years old and has been admitted to A&E with severe abdominal pain. She is accompanied by both parents. It is the policy of the unit to do a pregnancy test with all females of child bearing age who are admitted with abdominal pain. You are the nurse allocated to Constance.

Constance's parents have requested that they are informed of all tests and results and agree that one of them will stay with her at all times. When you asked for a urine sample for the pregnancy test, both parents appeared shocked at the idea that their daughter might be sexually active and only agree to the test with great reluctance. The pregnancy test was positive. You tell Constance this at a point when her parents are talking to the senior nurse. She begs you not to tell her parents.

Balancing patient confidentiality and safety

You are on your community placement and have been visiting patient, George White, with an occupational therapist. The occupational therapist has been working with George since his discharge home from hospital.

George was admitted to hospital following a fall at home where he had sustained cuts and bruises. He was found by a neighbour who does his shopping. George lives alone and has two married daughters who do not live locally.

During one of these visits, George discloses that he has been having falls but 'never that bad'. Further discussion reveals that he has had three to four falls in the past year but he 'managed' without hurting himself too badly. When asked if he had told anyone else, for example, his GP or his family, he told you that he does not wish his GP or daughters to know. He says they would worry about him and would think that he is not coping on his own. He also says firmly that he wishes to continue living at home.

Confidentiality: What It Means and Why It Matters

The rule of confidentiality in healthcare can be traced back to the Hippocratic Oath and appears in professional and international codes. It is described as follows:

> Confidentiality is present when one person discloses information to another, whether through words or other means, and the person to whom the information is disclosed pledges (implicitly or explicitly) not to divulge that information to a third party without the confider's permission. (Beauchamp & Childress 2009: 304)

Such information is considered private and is disclosed in a context of trust and confidence. Confidentiality is emphasised in both the Nursing and Midwifery Council (NMC) (2008a) and Health Professions Council (HPC) (2008) Codes. In the past, there was scepticism that the rhetoric and reality of confidentiality in healthcare practice did not match. In the 1980s, for example, Mark Siegler argued that confidentiality was 'a decrepit concept'. His research demonstrated that so many people (in the case of one patient, seventy five people) had access to patient records that it became meaningless (Beauchamp & Childress 2009: 303). It is important that patients know who can have legitimate access to their medical information and why.

There are exceptions to confidentiality. In the case of a child confidentiality may be broken, with the consent of the parents or the child if the child is Fraser/Gillick competent, that is deemed capable of making an informed decision. The professional is also obliged to consider at all times what is in the best interests of the child. This is particularly important if a child or young person asks to talk to you in confidence and you think this might be about a safeguarding or child protection issue. The child may ask you to promise to keep what they say secret and not tell their parents or anyone else. You cannot promise this as in safeguarding issues, you must report what you have been told to an appropriate person.

Confidentiality can always be broken with the consent of the patient or to others concerned with the provision of care to the patient. It can also be broken if there is a Court Order as you must obey the law. Other circumstances where confidential information can be shared include where breaking confidentiality is in the public interest. An important case illustrating this concept is *W. v Edgell* explained below.

W v Edgell [1990] 1 All ER 835

A prisoner, in a secure hospital, convicted of multiple killings, sought a review of his case, applying for a transfer to a regional secure unit. Dr Edgell, a psychiatrist instructed on behalf of the prisoner, made a report which was unfavourable. As a result the prisoner abandoned the application for review. He was nonetheless entitled to a routine review of his case. Dr Edgell, who was aware that his report would not be included in the patient's notes, sent a copy to the medical director of the hospital. It also came to the attention of the Home Secretary. The prisoner sued for breach of confidentiality. His case was dismissed.

$\rightarrow$

> There is one consideration which...weights the balance of public interest decisively in favour of disclosure....Where a man has committed multiple killings under the disability of serious mental illness, decisions which may lead directly or indirectly to his release from hospital should not be made unless a responsible authority is properly able to make an informed judgment...[A psychiatrist who believes that a decision might be made] on the basis of inadequate information and with a real risk of consequent danger to the public is entitled to take such steps as are reasonable ... to communicate his concern to the responsible authorities.
>
> Per Bingham LJ.

The law can require the breaking of confidentiality in relation to the incidence of certain diseases such as measles, mumps or TB. This is now governed by the *Public Health (Control of Disease) Act 1984* s.2A (inserted by the *Health and Social Care Act 2001* s.60) which allows the Minister to make appropriate regulations.

Clearly, the above exceptions are complex and often arise in difficult situations. Overall, you need to maintain the patient's confidentiality but this does not mean withholding appropriate information within the health- care team. It means not sharing information with people who do not need to know and who have no legal or ethical right to know. The right to confidentiality is also enforced by Article 8 of the *European Convention on Human Rights* which protects a person's right to respect for privacy and family life (discussed in more detail below p. 97).

Ethical aspects

The rule of confidentiality in healthcare is supported by two types of ethical argument: a consequentialist argument; and arguments from autonomy and individual rights (Beauchamp & Childress 2009). Consequentialist arguments involve weighing up the benefits and harms from maintaining or breaching confidentiality. This can be thought of in terms of the principles of beneficence and non-maleficence. The benefits of maintaining confidentiality relate to the likelihood that a promise of confidentiality will result in patients sharing information that contributes to improvements in their health or in the health of others. There are, of course, some risks also for patients if they share information that suggests they are putting themselves or others in danger. Professionals may then have to report the details to another authority, for example, mental health or social services. If, however, patients believe that professionals are not to be trusted with confidential information they may withhold it jeopardising their own health or the health of others.

Arguments from autonomy and individual rights support patients' right to confidentiality. The question 'whose information is it anyway?' is pertinent here. Information belongs to, and should be within the control of, the patient. Maintaining confidentiality or informational privacy is an important part of respect for autonomy. Whereas the first type of argument focuses on a broader weighing of benefits and harms for the patient and others, the autonomy arguments focus on the individual rights of the patient. The latter argument, in particular, reminds you not to abuse your privileged access to private patient information. However, the consequentialist argument cautions against promising absolute confidentiality. Patients may disclose information to you that suggests they or others may be at risk and, in these circumstances, it is vital that appropriate action is taken. Providing clear and honest information about the standards of, and exceptions to, confidentiality to patients is essential so they do not feel disrespected, manipulated or misled. This is important in maintaining trusting professional/patient relationships.

Legal aspects

Confidentiality is viewed as a fundamental aspect of professional practice that is underpinned by human rights. Indeed, the *European Convention of Human Rights*, Article 8 states that:

- ▶ Everyone has the right to respect for his private and family life, his home and his correspondence
- ▶ There shall be no interference by a public authority with the exercise of this right except such as is in accordance with the law and is necessary in a democratic society in the interests of national security, public safety or the economic well-being of the country, for the prevention of disorder or crime, for the protection of health or morals, or for the protection of the rights and freedoms of others.

The European Court of Human Rights has generally needed to consider the extent of the duty of confidentiality in relation to the right to free speech protected by Article 10. Article 10 is interpreted on the basis of 'whether there was an over-riding public interest in publishing the contested information, when to do so was harmful' to an individual. (*Leempoel & SAA ED Cine Revuev Belgium Hudoc (2006) para 79* cited Harris et al. 2009: 486) In such cases, the courts are required to carry out a balancing act between the rights of privacy and the right of freedom of expression.

In *Z v Finland (1998)* 25 EHRR 371 the European Court was asked to find that Z's right to privacy under Article 8 had been breached when her HIV status was disclosed, without her consent. Her husband was on trial for attempted manslaughter having engaged in sexual acts when he knew that he was HIV positive. He refused to give evidence. Z's medical records were seized and her doctor ordered to give evidence to try to establish when the husband was first aware of his condition. Z's identity was disclosed in the judgment of the Finnish Court of Appeal which was faxed to the press. Z complained to the European Court of Human Rights that her right of privacy under Article 8 had been violated. The Court had to decide whether or not the disclosure was '*necessary.*' It was decided that the public interest in bringing a criminal trial justified the breach of privacy The Court accepted that although respect for medical confidentially is a vital principle, disclosure can exceptionally be justified.

> any state measures compelling communication or disclosure of such information without the consent of the patient call for the most careful scrutiny on the part of the Court. (*Z v Finland (1998) 25 EHRR 371* at para. 96)

In Chapter 1, you had the opportunity to learn about common law and statute law. This duty of confidence is derived from common law (the decisions of the Courts) and statute law (which is passed by Parliament).In common law, the duty of confidentiality arises where information is given in circumstances which import a condition of confidentiality. The law of confidentiality is derived from a number of areas of common law. It reflects the fact that individuals have a right to expect that any information given to a healthcare professional is used only for the purpose for which it was given and will not be disclosed without permission. Doctors are not immune from this either. They are required to 'treat patients as individuals and respect their dignity ... respect patients' rights to confidentiality' (General Medical Council 2009). We are also reminded that information must be disclosed, in line with the law of the country in which we are practising if we believe someone may be at risk of harm.

With children and young people there is the additional complication that they do not legally become adults until they are 18. However, they are allowed to give consent from the age of 16 and younger children can do so if they are deemed competent, Gillick competent, to do so. This obviously has implications for confidentiality as a competent child or young person has the same right to confidentiality as an adult.

The right to confidentiality is also protected by the provisions of the *Data Protection Act 1998* which governs the way in which, the purposes for which and the storage of, data is obtained. The statutory requirements and the need to keep accurate and detailed records is discussed in more detail in Chapter 1 at pp. 17–18.

Professional aspects

Before any decision can be made, it is important to consider the clauses of the codes in accordance to the HPC and that of the NMC in relation to confidentiality.

The HPC Standards states that 'You must treat information about service users as confidential and use it only for the purposes they have provided it for' (HPC 2008 para. 2). The need to respect other people's confidentiality is also emphasised in the NMC code (2008a: paras 5–7) which state that:

▶ You must respect people's right to confidentiality.
▶ You must ensure that people are informed about how and why information is shared by those who will be providing their care.
▶ You must disclose information if you believe someone may be at risk of harm, in line with the law of the country in which you are practising.

The NMC's 'Guidance for the care of older people' (NMC 2008b) sets out key principles to enable nurses to 'think through the issues so that nurses could apply professional expertise and judgement' (ibid: 6) to safeguard the interest of older people in their care.

One of the issues identified concerns the need for nurses to be aware of any situation where 'there is the potential for confidentiality to be breached' (ibid: 25). The Guidance suggests that care should be taken that 'personal information and details are not disclosed to other people in your care, relatives, visitors or others who are not involved in the care process' (ibid: 25).

Application to Scenarios

'Don't tell my parents': a nurse's dilemma

In the case of Constance, the nurse was able to get Constance's consent to tell her parents that she was pregnant. Her parents were shocked and angry but because the nurse told them rather than Constance, they were able to express this to the nurse before they spoke to their daughter. At the point of discharge, Constance and her parents knew what her options were and were going home to discuss what to do.

Constance is 14 years old and therefore below the age of consent. You need to think about whether or not you should raise this with Constance and her family. Although legally 16 is still the age of consent, the norms of British society have changed and a lot of young people below the age of 16 are sexually active. You need to make a judgement about whether raising this point would help the situation. One thing that you do need to consider, however, is whether or not Constance was coerced into having sex. If you have any suspicions about this at all, you should raise them with an appropriate person. You also need to think about the age of the father of Constance's child. If he is much older than her it raises questions of exploitation, sexual abuse and paedophilia.

Ethical issues

Regarding the ethical dimensions of this scenario there is a need to respect Constance's right to autonomy. You have no reason to assume that she is not competent (Gillick competent) to make a rational decision, in this case not to tell her parents, even though you may not agree with it. You also need to think about the consequences of not telling her parents in relation to Constance's health. Young, single mothers need good ante-natal care to ensure the health of the baby and their own health. Ante-natal care needs to start early in the pregnancy and Constance needs to be supported psychologically if she decides to continue with the pregnancy. If she decides to terminate the pregnancy, she will also need physical care and psychological support. Ideally, this will be given by health professionals working in partnership with Constance and her parents so you need to consider whether withholding information from her parents will be in Constance's best long-term interests.

An additional argument not discussed earlier relates to the principle of justice: is Constance being treated in a just or fair way? In our society, are young people treated in the same way as adults or are their opinions not taken seriously? There have been situations where a child's right to refuse treatment has been overridden by their parents or health professionals acting in a paternalistic way. Might, for example, professionals think that the child is not Fraser/Gillick competent just because she is not agreeing with them! (For a more detailed discussion of this problem, see Chapter 4.)

In this case, other considerations are the short-term and long-term consequences (consequentialist argument) of not telling Constance's parents that she is pregnant. In the short term it is tempting to see it as more beneficial not to tell them as she is asking you not to and you think that they might be upset. However, in the longer term, child health and children's nursing are based on partnership with the children and their families. You could argue, therefore, that in the longer term, it would be more beneficent to tell Constance's parents now and work together to resolve the situation. Not telling them will also mean that you are jeopardising their being able to trust you and endangering the ethical principle of truth telling. On a very practical level, they are going to see that she is pregnant as soon as her body changes with the pregnancy.

Legal issues

There is a need to make a judgement about Constance's ability to make a rational decision about her health and a decision will have to be made about whether or not she is Fraser/Gillick competent. It is important to be open with Constance regarding professional obligations of confidentiality so that she is aware of exceptions to the rule. In practice, the assessment of Constance's competence is done by senior members of the healthcare team who will reach this decision after discussing the situation with her. If you were the nurse, your role would be to share what Constance has told you with the team and to support Constance in what will be a very difficult situation.

The literature on the safeguarding of children is clear that the interests and welfare of the child are paramount. This has also been critically discussed (Wainwright & Gallagher 2010). In such situations, it may not always be clear how to achieve this. Constance is part of a family unit and children's nursing is based on the philosophy of Family Centred Care and working in partnership with children, young people and their families. At first sight, the situation seems to an irresolvable dilemma: either you keep Constance's secret and risk alienating the parents; or you tell her parents and risk alienating Constance. Constance has the right to be heard (UN Convention on the Rights of the Child). She also has a right to privacy and dignity (DH). This may conflict with the parental rights and obligations of her parents as Constance is under 16 which in the UK is the age at which a child has capacity to make its own healthcare decisions (*Family Law Reform Act 1969*). There are no clear cut answers in this situation as both parties have ethical and legal rights and responsibilities.

Professional issues

Both the HPC (2008) and NMC (2008) Standards emphasise the importance of maintaining confidentiality. Exceptional circumstances when it is justifiable to disclose confidential information are when: someone may be at risk of harm or in line with the law of the country in which you are practising or when a person consents to you sharing this information with another person.

The best solution appears to have been found as the nurse negotiated with Constance and obtained her consent to tell her parents. As discussed above, whether she continues with the pregnancy or decides to have a termination, her body will change and she will need physical and psychological care. Should the nurse assume the role of Constance's advocate, she would be speaking on her behalf and representing her interests.

As a health professional your role is to work in partnership with the child or young person and their family. They will continue to be a family unit after your involvement with them has ended so at all times, think about what is best for everyone and how you can best offer support.

Balancing patient confidentiality and safety

In George's case, a duty of care has arisen whereby the health professionals are expected by George to hold the information in confidence. George has disclosed that he has had several falls in the past year. He insists that he has managed and that he does not want his family or his doctor to be told about it. In the actual case, the professional maintained George's confidentiality and did not share information with his family. However, she did share information with other team members involved with George.

It is easy to respond to George and reassure him that he would be fine and that you would respect his need for confidentiality. But, what could be the implications? Given his history of falls, it is likely that he would experience future falls. In the UK about a third of older people aged over 65 living in the community fall each year (Yardley et al. 2006). This risk increases with about 45 per cent of older adults aged 80 or more who live in the community fall each year (Department of Health 2009). Although not all falls are preventable, it is possible to minimise the risks involved thus reducing the risk of injurious falls. It is important to involve George in the decision making about fall prevention and interventions. This relates to respecting him as an autonomous individual.

Falling can put a strain on the family and is an independent predictor of admission to a nursing home (Tinetti & Williams 1997). As his previous fall was injurious , resulting in him being hospitalised, he may already be aware of what the potential long-term consequences might be and this might explain his reluctance to tell his family and his GP about his falls.

So, what are the ethical, legal and professional issues that might arise from this scenario?

Ethical issues

There are several ethical issues that are relevant in the above scenario. These include benefits versus harm, respectfulness, autonomy and confidentiality. Based on the 'four principles approach' (see Chapter 1) you can deduce that 'respect for autonomy' is highly relevant when you consider if George is autonomous and if his autonomy should be respected. If George has capacity and is considered autonomous, it can be argued that he should decide whether or not to tell his family about his fall history. We need to respect George's right to hold his views about what can be disclosed and what choices he wishes to make.

It is important also to consider the short-term and long-term consequences of maintaining confidentiality and of not doing anything about his falls. All being well, his leg wound will heal in the next few weeks. George may feel confident about getting on with his daily activities. However, given the knowledge that he has had several falls in the past year, from a long-term perspective, it is very likely that he will experience more falls and if injurious, he would have reduced mobility, and over a long period of time, his quality of life would be affected. Withholding information from his GP and family may deprive George of their potential support and advice if they knew of his falls, such as directing him to the right type of falls services available in the community.

Another related issue to consider is that of trust. The NMC (2008a) states that people in your care must be 'able to trust you with their health and wellbeing' (ibid: 1). If you have disclosed what George has asked you not to, your action could compromise the nurse–patient relationship as we know the key to such relationship is trust. George needs to first trust that you will treat him with respect and recognise his autonomy. At the same time he needs to be able to make the right decision while you, as a health professional attempt to walk a fine line between trying to influence him and assuming control, thus causing an imbalance in the nurse–patient relationship.

It is important to be aware that the way we perceive George may be misconstrued as 'ageist' in that we could see him as part of a generation of older people, as incompetent and dependent. Holding a stereotypical perception of older people can compromise your professional approach and value judgement. Nurses have in the past been accused of speaking with the older person's relatives or 'talking over the head' of the older person ignoring the rights and respect of the older person.

Where George is concerned, it is important that the professional is aware that he is at risk of falling. To prevent him from sustaining further harm as a result of an injurious fall would be one of the goals of nursing. However, George, like other individuals, may weigh the social risks against perceived health risks, in order to decide which is deemed the lesser of two evils. Should he disclose his falls to his GP and his daughters or should he continue to risk falling? Proctor (2002) identifies a dynamic tension between risk and safety in the care of older adults. It is thus not surprising that older adults may be reluctant to inform their family members or friends about their health and/or social problems (Horton 2006). Kingston (1998) found 87 of the 107 older adults in his study sample had not discussed falls they had suffered, either with their family members or with a friend. Other research also found that older adults are reluctant about seeking help from their children, or disclosing their need for help (Horton 2006). Ballinger and Payne (2002) stressed the need for care professionals to adopt a person-centred approach and value the personal contribution of an older person.

A balance should be struck between protecting older people from harm and allowing them as much personal freedom as possible (Gastmans in Hughes 2010). Although it is important that professionals respect a person's rights, it must be borne in mind that it does not mean that they would always have to give priority to that individual's rights over everything else (Rowson 2007). While George might wish to exercise his right to confidentiality, the professional would be breaching his right only when there are no stronger countervailing ethical or legal considerations that justify doing so.

Legal issues

In George's case, as an adult he has the right to privacy as well as the right to control access to his personal health information. Although George may have protection by virtue of Article 8 of the *European Convention on Human Rights*, little protection is available under English law. Generally a right to confidentiality will be enforced when it is in the public interest that this should be so and the patient would suffer detriment from disclosure. The issue facing the courts is illustrated by the following case.

X v Y [1988] 2 All ER 648

The names of two practising doctors who were being treated for AIDS had been obtained by a local newspaper which was proposing to publish the names. In balancing the important public interest in freedom of the press with the interests of the individuals concerned Mr Justice Rose said '... in my judgement those public interests are substantially outweighed when measured against the public interests in relation to loyalty and, confidentiality ... .'

An injunction was granted to prevent publication.

It is unlikely that George would seek a remedy from the courts but it must be remembered that breach of confidentiality is forbidden by the professional Codes. Were a complaint made to the courts, the rules previously discussed in this chapter, particularly in relation to Article 8, would govern the decision reached by the court.

Professional issues

From a professional perspective, it is not acceptable that healthcare professionals discuss matters related to the people in their care outside the care setting. Should you discuss details of a practice situation with another colleague, you need to ensure that this discussion does not take place in public where you may be overheard. The professional might make a written record of what was disclosed by George in George's case notes, in which case it is critical that they do not leave any records unattended where they might be accessed by unauthorised persons.

Vanlaere and Gastmans (2007) argued that nurses' solicitude for patients and their well-being is necessary in the care provided, and to make it effective, nurses must be knowledgeable and skilful. In George's case, the nurse would need to be knowledgeable about the risk of falling and how the gendered perspective might deter an older man like George to be more open about his own risk of falling (Horton 2007). Older men perceive themselves to be 'rational individuals' to legitimise their falls since their experiences were found to be more discrediting (Horton 2002). The desire to remain independent can place an older person like George at odds with family members. Porter (1994: 59) found that widows often reported their children giving 'unsolicited precautionary advice or directions' such as you 'shouldn't be doing that [lawn mowing] anymore'. The notion that older people may be exposing themselves to risk, 'doing too much', can be contentious within the family when the older parent and their adult children have opposing perceptions about how much was too much.

Conclusion

In this chapter you have been introduced to two scenarios focusing on the issue of confidentiality. Despite their age differences, both persons have the right to confidentiality. This is not, however, an absolute right and whichever approach we take as health professionals, will have serious implications for the individual, their family and ourselves. Our discussion has shown the relevance and importance of ethical, legal and professional perspectives.

In the first scenario, the issue of confidentiality is complex because of the age of the patient. It was further complicated by the involvement of the family who, to that point, were probably used to be being fully involved in any discussions about their daughter's health. Although it is quite clear that it is the welfare of the child that comes first, in this situation, health professionals have to decide how that can best be achieved. The ultimate aim of any decision would be to support the child, young person and their family and to work with them to achieve this. It will take a lot of skill to achieve this but the long-term benefit to Constance and her family makes it essential

In the second scenario, the issue of confidentiality is equally complex as it involves issues of trust, risk management, autonomy and ageism. Despite his age, health professionals need to recognise that George is capable of making his decision and is aware of his risk of falling, and at the same time strike a balance of power within the nurse–patient relationship without compromising the quality of care and outcomes. As Rowson (2007) has alluded to, professionals may be regarded as having an obligation to balance some of the rights of individual patients against other considerations.

References

Ballinger, C. & Payne, S. (2002) The construction of the risk of falling among and by older people. *Ageing and Society*, 22, 305–324.

Beauchamp, T.L. & Childress, J.F. (2009) *Principles of Biomedical Ethics* (6th ed.). Oxford University Press, New York.

Department of Health (2009) *Falls and Fractures: Effective Interventions in Health and Social Care*. London, Department of Health.

Gastmans, C. (2010) 'Clinical-ethical consideration on the use of physical restraint' in Hughes, R. (Ed.) *Rights, Risk and Restraint-Free Care of Older People*. Jessica Kingsley Publishers, London, pp. 106–119.

General Medical Council (2009) *Confidentiality: Guidance*. General Medical Council, UK.

Harris, D.J., O'Boyle, M., Dates, E.P. & Buckley, C.M. (2009) *Law of the European Convention on Human Rights* (2nd ed.). Oxford University Press, Oxford.

Health Professions Council (2008) *Standards of Conduct, Performance and Ethics*. HPC, London.

Horton, K. (2002) *Gender and Falls: Perceptions of Older People and their Family Members*. Unpublished PhD thesis. University of Surrey.

Horton, K. (2006) 'Balancing Risk and Independence' in Godin, P. (Ed.) *Risk and Nursing Practice*. Palgrave Macmillan , Basingstoke, pp. 150–162.

Horton, K. (2007) Gender and the risk of falling: a sociological approach. *Journal of Advanced Practice*, 57(1), 69–76.

Kingston, P. (1998) *Older People and Falls: A Randomised Control Trial on Health Visitor Intervention*. Unpublished Ph D thesis. Keele University.

Nursing and Midwifery Council (2008a) *The Code: Standards of Conduct, Performance and Ethics for Nurses and Midwives*. Nursing and Midwifery Council, London.

Nursing and Midwifery Council (2008b) *Guidance for the Care of Older People*. Nursing and Midwifery Council, London.

Porter, E.J. (1994) Older widows' lived experience of 'risk': how they articulated the risks they experienced and ways in which they attempted to reduce these risks. *Advances in Nursing Science*, 17(2), 54–65.

Procter, S. (2002) Whose evidence? Agenda setting in multiprofessional research: observations from a case-study. *Health, Risk and Society*, 4(1), 43–59.

Rowson, R. (2007) Nurses' difficulties with rights. *Nursing Ethics,* 14(6), 838–840.

Tinetti, M.E. & Williams, C.S. (1997) Falls, injuries due to falls, and the risk of admission to a nursing home. *New England Journal of Medicine*, 337(18), 1279–84.

Vanlaere, L. & Gastmans, C. (2007) Ethics in nursing education: learning to reflect on care practices. *Nursing Ethics*, 14(6), 758–766.

Wainwright, P. & Gallagher, A. (2010) Understanding general pracitioners' conflicts of interests and the paramountcy principle in safeguarding children. *Journal of Medical Ethics,* 36, 302–305.

Yardley, L., Donovan-Hall, M., Francis, K, & Todd, C. (2006) Older people's views of advice about falls prevention: a qualitative study. *Health Education Research,* 21(4), 508–517.

Chapter 7
Justice and fairness

Helen Allan

The introductory chapter to this book defined justice in terms of fairness and entitlement. In a context of resource constraints in healthcare; debates continue as to who should have access to what treatments and on what basis. Should, for example, *in vitro* fertilisation be available to lesbian and single women? Is it fair for postcodes to determine the allocation of resources such as new drugs for cancer therapies? Should people with unhealthy lifestyles have access to scarce organs when they require a transplant? On what basis do you allocate resources, including your time, to patients and others when these are limited?

This chapter focuses on two practice scenarios which concern individual entitlements. These entitlements can easily be violated in everyday practice and such situations may present you, as a professional, with difficult ethical decisions and raise questions about the meaning of justice and fairness in everyday practice. The meaning of justice in the context of healthcare will be clarified before applying these theoretical points to the scenarios. There will be opportunities for you to think about your responses to the scenarios and discuss them with colleagues. The two scenarios invite you, then, to reflect on issues relating to justice and fairness in healthcare and to consider responses that are ethical, legal and professional.

As you read the scenarios I suggest you keep two questions in mind:

- If you were the professional concerned in the scenario, what would you do?
- Why would you respond this way? Refer to relevant ethical, legal and professional concepts and arguments that could support your action.

Scenarios

Responding to racism in care

You are an overseas-trained nurse, registered with the Nursing and Midwifery Council (NMC), and have come from Ghana to work in the UK. You go to help a student, Susan, who is working with an elderly resident in the home. You are Susan's mentor. Susan is helping the resident to wash and dress. Both the student and the resident are white British. When you enter the room the resident says: 'I don't want any black bastard' and she makes it clear she does not want you to help with her care.

Fairness in offering learning support to students

You are a mentor working with students in a post-anaesthetic care unit (PACU). You have two operating department practitioner pre-registration students, Samina and Dennis, allocated to you during their placement. You have found Samina easier to work with than Dennis. Samina is quiet and has an easy manner with patients and colleagues. You find Dennis more challenging as he asks a lot of questions of you and other members of the team. In purely personal terms, you like Samina more than Dennis. So far you have been able to give them equal time in your role as their mentor but you are worried that your preference for Samina may become obvious to Dennis. You are also concerned that your preference may influence the assessment of their practice.

Ethical aspects

Justice is something you might take for granted in 21st century England. Unless you have felt a sense of injustice, you might not be aware of justice. There are particular challenges in healthcare regarding justice. People from every class and region in the UK are healthier and living longer than ever before (DH 2010a). However, inequalities persist as a report in February 2010, the Marmot Review (DH 2010b), showed. Despite impressive social, economic and health improvements in the UK, not everyone is able to share the benefits of these improvements.

Successive governments believe that it is essential that everyone is empowered and encouraged to accept their entitlement . This involves a fair and just distribution of resources among the citizens of the UK. The Marmot review (DH 2010b) stressed that tackling health inequalities was a matter of social justice, with real economic benefits and savings. Repeated initiatives have tried to tackle health and social inequalities. One such is the Healthy Places, Healthy Lives Initiative (DH

2010d) which will encourage local leadership on the health inequalities agenda and share learning. The intention is that health inequalities becomes everybody's business. Justice is often discussed in relation to the bigger issues to do with society, health and inequalities or distribution (see, for example, Pearce et al. 2010).

There are different philosophical views, and different types, of justice. John Locke, for example, argued that justice is a natural law in society, that is, it derives from nature and has validity everywhere – it almost becomes taken for granted (Giddens 2008). Other philosophers, such as Thomas Hobbes, have argued that justice only exists when there are public, enforceable and authoritative rules. Justice is whatever those rules forbid regardless of their relationship to morality and any infraction of these rules requires punishment. In the 18th Century, for example, a 12-year-old could have been found guilty and sentenced to hanging for stealing. We would think this punishment unethical and unfair today but the boy had broken the law, and in society's eyes needed to be punished. Justice was considered to be upheld, at that time, through his punishment.

In a principle-based approach to healthcare ethics, justice is one of the four principles considered to underpin ethical practice in healthcare (Beauchamp & Childress 2009). Justice encompasses society's expectations of what is fair and right and is considered overwhelmingly important (Rawls 1999). Notions of fairness and of right and wrong have strong emotional appeal for individuals (Wolpert 2008). Fairness and justice are not, of course, just the concern of individuals. Groups, previously disadvantaged and marginalised, have worked together to attain rights comparable with those of other groups. Think, for example, of the fight to obtain justice for women in the UK at the beginning of the 20th century (http://news.bbc.co.uk) or for black people in the USA in the 1950s and 1960s (http://www.infoplease.com). At the time of writing you might also think of the right to maternity care and education for women and girls in Afghanistan (http://www.medicalnewstoday.com).

Such considerations are related to rights-based approaches to justice in healthcare. These approaches ask the question: is there a right to healthcare? Beauchamp and Childress (2009) argue that there are two responses to this question which are similar to Rawls' principles of justice above. The first response suggests that healthcare can be viewed as similar to other needs which governments protect, such as education and safety. Threats to health therefore are of equal magnitude as threats from crime, war and pollution. The second response posits that rights to healthcare are about fair opportunity and poor health results in disease and disability. The former increases individual chances of fair opportunity for action. However, the difficulty of these responses is that healthcare is expensive and societies cannot or choose not to fund all healthcare. Beauchamp and Childress (2009: 260) suggest that another question might be: is there a right to a minimum standard of healthcare? If you answer yes, the advantage of this response is that it guarantees basic healthcare for all on a premise of equal access while allowing unequal additional purchases by individual initiative. The questions of whether there are rights or minimum rights to healthcare are what politicians from both the left and the right in the UK argue about in respect of health services.

For the ancient Greek philosopher, Plato (Waterfield 1984), the presence of justice signified proper, harmonious relationships in society. Just persons are in the right place, doing their best and giving the precise equivalent of what they receive from others. You can, however, only act justly if you are reflective or wise. Banks and Gallagher (2009: 168) argue that justice comprises a 'disposition to act fairly in relation to individuals to whom one has an obligation and to act in a way that promotes and reflects just social arrangements'. Reflecting through exercises in this book on real life scenarios is a way of developing a reflective ability and habit in practice.

Several forms or types of justice are identified in the bioethics literature. Beauchamp and Childress (2009), for example, distinguish among distributive justice, criminal and rectificatory justice. Arries (2009) refers to distributive justice, procedural justice and interactional justice. The forms of justice most relevant to our discussion here are: *distributive justice* and *interactional justice*. Distributive justice concerns the distribution of resources, goods or benefits and burdens within a society. In considering distributive justice, we need to consider what goods and on what basis or principles are they distributed? Is it on the basis of wealth, power, respect or a combination of these things? You might think that fairness or justice is what you are entitled to through your own hard work (Nozick 1974) or you might think that everyone is entitled to a fair share of society's goods and resources depending on their ability to work *and* their contribution (Rawls 1999).

In addition to effort and contribution, Beauchamp and Childress (2009) suggest a range of material principles that might justify what people might justly receive. These include: to each an equal share;

to each according to need; to merit; and according to free market exchanges. When you consider access to scarce healthcare resources, you might consider the implications of each of these principles: what would the implications be of everyone being entitled to an equal share of healthcare resources? Should those in most need receive the most healthcare? Or perhaps those considered to have more merit, for example, people in high status positions? Regarding free market exchanges, those who can afford to pay have access to private health-care and can jump the waiting list. Is this fair? Should people be per-mitted to buy organs if others are willing to sell them? Also, should healthcare be restricted to citizens of a particular nation? These considerations are familiar to us in healthcare as access to health-care and health inequalities have been criticisms of all healthcare systems (Beauchamp & Childress 2009). As the demand for health-care resources increases and their availability is limited, ethical decision making regarding who should get what and why becomes unavoidable.

Interactional justice, according to Arries (2009: 149), 'is viewed as a distinct construct of justice and emphasizes the quality of the interpersonal treatment people receive in the implementation of just procedures'. Arries focuses his discussion of interactional justice on student experiences with clinical staff but it is possible to widen its scope to other areas. In relation to students, Arries emphasises the degree of respect and politeness they are afforded by staff and the fairness and truthfulness of evaluation methods. Interactional justice relates primarily to the quality of relationships or 'social exchange' between individuals. Arries conducted an empirical study in South Africa with 98 nursing students to identify their perceptions of inter-actional justice during clinical placements. He used a 14-item ques-tionnaire to measure student perceptions of interactional justice and found that students rated their experience with staff nurses in prac-tice as 'interactionally unjust' (Arries 2009: 156). Interestingly, the longer students worked in a clinical placement the more likely they were to perceive staff to be fair and to develop relationships that were more trusting.

This section has focused on some ethical and philosophical approaches to justice and fairness which are relevant to healthcare and health professionals. It has also given you some resources on the inter-net for further reading. I next consider legal and professional aspects of justice and fairness.

Legal aspects

In England and Wales, *Magna Carta (1215)* is arguably one of the earliest sources of justice and fairness. The Charter:

- set out the rights of various classes of the community according to their different needs,
- provided that no-one should be punished except by judgment of his peers or the law,
- ensured that justice should be denied to no-one.

From 1215 the legal system gradually developed ways to protect individuals from injustice. Over the centuries in all parts of the United Kingdom the role of government has become more intrusive into the life of citizens as society has become more complex, the government assuming responsibility for welfare issues such as the provision of healthcare, housing, education, social care, to meet the needs of the population. The possibility that such power could be abused led to the development of the process of judicial review in relation to administrative decision making. The process allows an administrative decision, for example, how resources should be allocated, to be challenged on the grounds of:

- illegality because the action goes beyond that authorised by a statute or interferes with basic rights or the decision maker has taken irrelevant matters into account;
- unreasonableness or irrationality when the decision is '... so outrageous in its defiance of logic or of accepted moral standards that no sensible person ... could have arrived at it' (per Lord Diplock in *In re the Council of Civil Service Unions and Others (England)* [1985] AC 374 at 410–411 also referred to as 'the GCHQ case.');
- disproportionality when the decision cannot be justified and/or alternatives have not been considered.

The process of judicial review is, however, complex and expensive.

In the context of health and social care, legal challenges have often been brought against decisions relating to the allocation of resources alleging that the decision is unreasonable. The following two cases show you how the courts have tried to explain how such decisions may be unreasonable.

R v Secretary of State for Social Services and others ex [p. Hincks (1980) 1 BMLR 93

Four patients had been waiting for orthopaedic surgery, the delay being caused because a new extension to their local hospital had been cancelled because of the cost. The patients said their need was reasonable and thus there was a duty, under the National Health Service Act 1987 s.3 to provide what was needed. The Act imposed a duty but did not say that justified an exception. The Court of Appeal held that the duty to provide services must be read as a duty to provide services '...to such extent as...necessary to meet all reasonable requirements such as can be provided within the resources available' (per Lord Denning MR).

R v Cambridge HA ex p. B [1995] 2 All ER 129

B, aged 10, had leukaemia. Her doctors advised that she only had six to eight weeks to live and further treatment would not be appropriate. A doctor in the USA agreed to give further treatment which he admitted was experimental and not standard. The Health Authority refused funding on the grounds that it would not be an effective use of resources. The Court of Appeal upheld the decision 'Difficult and agonizing judgements have to be made as to how a limited budget is best allocated to the maximum advantage of the maximum of patients. That is not a judgement which the court can make' (per Sir Thomas Bingham).

A challenge may be more likely to be successful if the decision has been made on the basis of a fixed policy. The policy should be sufficiently flexible to take account of the individual's need and to consider his/her views. The following case illustrates this point.

R v N W Lancashire H A ex p. A, D and G [2000] 2 FCR 525

A rigid policy against funding gender re-assignment surgery was held to be unlawful. While a decision that a particular treatment would not generally be funded could be lawful, it is essential that the individual's particular needs be taken into account.

In relation to the availability of drugs, the issue of cost as such is not always relevant. Of more importance is the potential benefit for the individual. The following cases provide you with examples of the very difficult decisions needed when the provision of very expensive life saving/life prolonging drugs has to be considered. This is illustrated by the following two cases.

R (Rogers) v Swindon NHS Primary Care Trust [2006] EWCA Civ 392

Mrs R, who had breast cancer, initially funded her own treatment with herceptin (at that time an unlicensed drug). When she could no longer afford the treatment she sought funding from the PCT. This was refused on the basis of a policy that the drug would only be provided if there were exceptional personal or clinical circumstances. The Court of Appeal held that such a policy could be lawful only if the policy makers had envisaged the kind of cases which might be exceptional. As this was not the case, the decision to refuse funding was unlawful. In other words, rationing may be lawful but the process must be open and transparent.

R (Otley) v Barking & Dagenham NHS PCT [2007] EWHC 1927 (Admin)

It was recommended that Mrs O should be treated with an anti-cancer drug (Avastin) . The Trust refused to fund the treatment on the basis that the use of the drug as part of a 'cocktail' had not been researched. The Court held that insufficient weight had been given to the fact that the proposed treatment was the only one available. Mrs O was entitled to have the chance of life.

The courts have made it clear that decision making in these difficult cases must be open and transparent. In this way the ethical principle of justice and fairness is upheld.

Another important way in which justice and fairness are upheld is by means of the laws relating to discrimination. Most recently the *Equality Act 2010* has reformed the law in England and Wales relating to all aspects of discrimination. The Act prohibits discrimination on the basis of *'protected characteristics'* namely:

- age,
- disability,
- gender re-assignment,
- marriage and civil partnership,
- race,
- religion or belief,

- sex,
- sexual orientation,
- pregnancy and maternity.

The *Equality Act 2010* is important for health professionals because it affects both access to and delivery of healthcare. All health professionals need to consider whether the care they deliver is accessible to everyone irrespective of any protected characteristic.

Professional aspects

When considering justice and fairness, there are specific aspects of the NMC Code (NMC 2008) and the HPC Standards (HPC 2008) which are relevant and must be considered. There are three behaviours and three attributes which seem pertinent to being just and fair as a health professional.

First, people have a right to be treated respectfully as individuals. Importantly, you must not discriminate in any way against those in your care – irrespective of their social, religious or ethnic background. (NMC Code paras 1–4; HPC Code para. 1)

Second, in relation to consent, while you must ensure that you gain consent before you begin any treatment or care, when considering justice and fairness, you must respect and support people's rights to accept or decline treatment and care and uphold people's rights to be fully involved in decisions about their care. You must be aware of the legislation regarding mental capacity, ensuring that people who lack capacity remain at the centre of decision making and are fully safeguarded. This is especially important given the inequalities in healthcare for elderly. (NMC Code paras 13–17; HPC Code para. 9)

In order to treat everyone equally, justly and fairly, you should maintain clear professional boundaries. (NMC Code paras 18–20; HPC Code para. 13).

The three attributes needed to meet the requirements of both codes considered here are to: be open and honest; act with integrity; uphold the reputation of your profession. You must demonstrate a personal and professional commitment to equality and diversity, thereby treating everyone equally, justly and fairly. Acting with integrity means you must be honest and open in your practice even if patients or their carers complain about your actions or those of others you work with. Lastly you must be impartial, that is not abuse your privileged position for your own ends and you must ensure that your professional judgment is not influenced by any commercial considerations.

Application to Scenarios

Responding to racism in care

This scenario was derived from data from a qualitative research project (Allan et al. 2004). The nurse explained in the study interview: 'I went in and I wanted to help a student with a resident; both the student and the resident were white. But the resident said "I don't want any black bastard". Quickly I had to handle it because if I didn't, it could escalate; it was embarrassing for me to be insulted in front of the student who I was mentoring. As the resident would not let us continue with our care, we stopped and I went and reported what had happened to the manager, who was white. She came and she said to the resident: "what did you call her, what did you call her?" I said: "Calm down, I was the one who was called 'Black bastard', you were not. First of all, am I not Black?" and everybody just went quiet. So then the manager said "Fine, okay, you are black, but what about the bastard?" So then I said "how do you know I am not a bastard?" and then people just started laughing, and from that time on I was accepted.

The scenario takes place in the older care sector but similar incidents are reported throughout the NHS (Allan, Cowie & Smith 2009). The patient is unfair to the nurse on the basis of her ethnicity. If you witnessed this incident while on placement, how would you have felt and would you have been able to do anything? Afterwards, whatever your ethnic background, would you have been able to discuss this incident with your mentor? What difference would ethnicity make to your discussion? Crucially, is using humour an appropriate response in such a situation? It is *one* response and in this situation, it seems that it may have contributed to the nurse feeling accepted. However, all health professionals who find themselves on the receiving end of insults, abuse or racism should be made aware of the complaints process.

The scenario illustrates justice and fairness as it focuses on the relationship between rights (to be treated fairly, with respect and dignity and not discriminated against) and the concepts of justice and fairness. In this scenario, the injustice is directed towards the professional herself and yet she responds generously and with a sense of humour. Scenario 1 illustrates how race and ethnicity can affect practice and raises ethical, legal and professional aspects of justice in healthcare relating to unfair discrimination on the basis of ethnicity and skin colour. The black nurse is initially prevented from doing her job by the patient because of her skin colour. We do not know why the patient has been racist and rude. Von Hippell suggests this may 'unintended racism' be due to brain atrophy (2007) or it may be a long held racist belief (Smith et al. 2006). Racism is based on personal values which may be unconscious (Allan & Smith 2008). Older people may have had less exposure to people from different cultures and their reaction may indicate a fear of the unknown. Nevertheless, unconscious or unwitting racism has as much effect on the person being discriminated against as deliberate racism.

Scenario 1 illustrates how racism affects the experience and delivery of care.

The distribution of resources and justice may be affected if the nurse who is discriminated against chooses to withdraw her labour (which she did temporarily). Equally the patient may have rights to resources which override her expressed values which are demonstrably racist. In Scenario 1 the underpinning rights of the professional to fair, respectful treatment are legally protected by the *Equality Act 2010*. Justice in this approach is enforced legally but as in Scenario 1 may not be enforced through a social contract between individuals.

In a national study of overseas nurses' experiences of racism and discrimination (Smith et al. 2006), different ways in which overseas-trained nurses described their experiences of being discriminated against were identified. Their descriptions illuminated two types of discrimination: overt and indirect discrimination. Overt discrimination appeared in the forms of blatant racism, xenophobia (fear of strangers) and apparent deliberate strategies to exclude or harm the overseas-trained nurse. Scenario 1 illustrates overt discrimination which is likely to be illegal if expressed in this way by an adult with capacity which may deny the individual his or her right to dignity.

Recent studies of violence in the NHS have found significant levels of colleague on colleague bullying (Ferns & Mccrabeau 2008) and of aggression on the part of patients towards health professionals, particularly in psychiatric, accident and emergency and maternity departments (Commission for Health Improvement (CHI), 2003; Healthcare Commission, 2006). Trade unions, professional organisations and human resources departments have become more aware that behaviours such as intimidation, public humiliation, offensive name-calling, social exclusion and unwanted physical contact have the potential to undermine the integrity and confidence of employees and reduce efficiency (Rayner & Höel 1997). People who have been attacked in these ways report that it affects them physically and mentally, with stress, depression and lowered self-esteem as the most common complaints. The *Equality Act 2010* is intended to provide more effective protection in relation to such behaviour but at the time of writing (January 2011) it is not yet possible to predict how effective the new law will be.

Ethical issues

Scenario 1 illustrates both distributive and restorative justice. Distributive justice is seen in the allocation of resources within the care home; the care the patient is entitled to, and the respect the nurse is due. Unfortunately these rights in this situation have become competing dues or rights. What is particularly insightful in the black nurse's response is how she avoids attacking the patient in return but uses the patient's own language to confront the disrespectful behaviour. The manager's response was to immediately demand aggressively what the patient had called the nurse. She seems to be hinting at retributive justice, that is punishment; this might prove difficult in situations where competing rights clash and especially in this case where the patient might be seen as vulnerable. The patient's values and beliefs about ethnicity shaped her racist behaviour towards the black nurse. The black nurse's values and beliefs about restorative or reparative justice, which focuses on the needs of the victim, shaped her response to an aggressive attack on her ethnic background albeit perhaps not as an individual attack, therefore making the behaviour xenophobic and not racist although still illegal. She believed that recognising the wrong and seeking to repair relationships was the right response. The result of the interaction was fair and just through the reflective and just behaviour of the black nurse. As highlighted above, health professionals in such situations should be aware of complaints processes within their organisation.

Legal issues

We have considered how legal frameworks have shaped and continue to shape societal responses to justice and fairness. In Scenario 1, the *Equality Act 2010* sets out the relevant law. (s.9) The Act spells out each person's fundamental rights irrespective of their racial origin and prevents discrimination in relation to those rights on any grounds.

Professional issues

Professionals are required in accord with guidelines the relevant Code of Conduct outlined above (NMC 2008; HPC 2008) to act professionally. In Scenario 1, the black nurse, manager and student are still required to act respectfully towards the patient unless accepted standards of behaviour are breached. In this case, some would argue that they were and that the patient has abrogated her right to care. However, the black nurse undertakes her own restorative justice and addresses the situation immediately while continuing to respect her patient. In so doing, she models professional and ethical behaviour to the student and manager.

Fairness in offering learning support to students

Scenario 2 may be less dramatic but raises a familiar and complex ethical choice around fair distribution of resources and rights to services, in this case, learning support. It illustrates distributive justice where the resource is the mentor's attention, time, feedback and perhaps more troublingly, attitude to Dennis, the second student. You might say, 'well this is just a personal dislike, what does it matter?' It matters because this is a professional relationship and the mentor is bound by a professional Code (NMC 2008, HPC 2008) to behave respectfully towards individuals, patients and staff, and to demonstrate a personal and professional commitment to equality and diversity, thereby treating everyone equally, justly and fairly. Acting with integrity means you must be honest and open in your practice. It is clear that the mentor is aware of the Code and her responsibility to act respectfully and with integrity otherwise she would not be reflecting on her feelings towards the two students at all. This in itself is ethical practice as Banks & Gallagher (2009: 168) indicate. They argue that justice comprises a 'disposition to act fairly in relation to individuals to whom one has an obligation and to act in a way that promotes and reflects just social arrangements'.

In this and similar scenarios, there are systems in place to help the mentor act ethically after considering distributive justice once she has reflected and reached an ethical decision. She can keep to her self-imposed rules which are fair and continue to support the student. By reflecting on her feelings towards Dennis, the mentor is being just and fair because she is recognising her part in the relationship and considering what she can change in her behaviour, not her attitude, to resolve the situation. In the actual situation, the mentor sought support from the link tutor to the ward area and discussed the best course of action with them. The mentor's main concern was that Dennis may feel that his entitlements have not been attended to. The mentor is properly focusing on being fair to everyone while recognising her personal feelings of liking or disliking.

Ethical issues

In Scenario 2, distributive justice is illustrated where the resource is the mentor's attention and time; each student appears to have competing rights but there are systems in place for a reflective professional to act justly. Interactional justice is what is most at stake, from an ethical perspective, in this scenario. If the mentor was unreflective, favouring one student (Samina) over another (Dennis), then it is possible that Dennis' experience may have been of interactional injustice.

Legal issues

In Scenario 2 both students have their rights upheld as the mentor continues to allocate her time and behave fairly to both. Had she done otherwise, the students may have been able to challenge her decisions.

Professional issues

Both scenarios describe the complexities of professional relationships and the work that professionals have to undertake as well as the skills they have to develop to act justly in professional practice. Above all, they show how important a reflective attitude is to professional and ethical practice. In both scenarios, the professionals act reflectively to bring about a just solution to a difficult ethical dilemma. In each situation, how the professionals respond will affect their future professional relationships with these individual students in Scenario 2 and the patient, the manager and the student in Scenario 1.

In Scenario 2, the mentor acts with personal and professional commitment to equality and diversity. She seeks to treat each student equally, justly and fairly. In both scenarios, the mentor and the black nurse act with integrity, remaining honest and open in their practice. In Scenario 1, this is open to everyone concerned. In Scenario 2, the openness is with herself in her reflections.

Conclusion

The scenarios discussed in this chapter have illustrated probably everyday occurrences in a multicultural workforce which is also a learning organisation where almost all trained staff have some role in teaching and supporting learners. This means that such issues as racism and being consistent and fair in one's dealings with learners have to be considered both by individuals and organisations if just and fair work environments are to be a reality. Unfortunately, the discussion in this chapter shows that the NHS workforce is not a just or fair one consistently, if at all (Ferns & Meerabeau 2008; Allan, Cowie & Smith 2009). Despite the legal and professional requirements to act justly and fairly, unfair and unjust behaviours are regularly reported. This indicates that such frameworks are not sufficient to ensure that people behave fairly or justly (Smith et al. 2006). In addition to legal and professional frameworks, individual responsibility for creating just and fair working environments is necessary. These scenarios show how individual reflective behaviours can meaningfully create ethical and therefore, fair and just behaviours.

References

Allan, H.T., Larsen, J., Bryan, K. & Smith, P. (2004) The social reproduction of institutional racism: internationally recruited nurses' experiences of the British Health Services. *Diversity in Health and Social Care,* 1(2),117–126.

Allan, H.T. & Smith, P.A. (2008) in Bryan K (Ed.) *Communication in Health Care.*

Allan, H.T., Cowie, H. & Smith, P.A. (2009) Overseas nurses' experiences of discrimination: a case of racist bullying. *Journal of Nursing Management,* 17, 898–906.

Arries E.J. (2009) Interactional Justice in student-staff nurses encounters. *Nursing Ethics,* 16(2), 146–160.

Banks, S. & Gallagher, A. (2009) *Ethics in Professional Life. Virtues for Health and Social Care.* Palgrave Macmillan, Basingstoke.

BBC News Q&A: Stephen Lawrence murder. BBC News. 5 May 2004. http://news.bbc.co.uk/1/hi/uk/3685733.stm (accessed 30 May 2011).

BBC News, http://news.bbc.co.uk/today/hi/today/newsid_9095000/9095090.stm Accessed 30 May 2011.

Beauchamp, T.L. & Childress (2009) *The Four Principles of Biomedical Ethics* (5th ed.). Oxford University Press, Oxford.

Commission for Health Improvement (CHI). (2003) *NHS National Staff Survey.* CHI, London.

DH (2010a) Health Inequalities. http://webarchive.nationalarchives.gov.uk/+/www.dh.gov.uk/en/Publichealth/Healthinequalities/index.htm (Accessed 1 December 2010).

DH (2010b) Fair Society, Healthy Lives. The Marmot review: strategic review of health inequalities Post-2010 (the Marmot Review) http://www.marmotreview.org/ (Accessed 1 December 2010).

DH (2010c) Health inequalities, everybody's business http://webarchive.nationalarchives.gov.uk/+/www.dh.gov.uk/en/MediaCentre/Pressreleasesarchive/DH_111274 (Accessed 1 December 2010).

Ferns, T. & Meerabeau, L. (2008) Verbal abuse experienced by nursing students. *Journal of Advanced Nursing,* 61(4), 436–444.

Giddens A. (2008) *Sociology* (5th ed.). Polity Press, Cambridge.

Healthcare Commission. (2006) *National Survey of NHS Staff 2005.* Commission for Healthcare Audit and Inspection, London.

Health Professions Council Standards of Conduct Performance and Ethics 2008 http://www.hpc-uk.org/publications/standards/index.asp?id=38

Infoplease, http://www.infoplease.com/spot/civilrightstimeline1.html, accessed 30 May 2011.

Medical News Today, http://www.medicalnewstoday.com/articles/195546.php, accessed 30 May 2011.

NMC Code of Conduct (2008) http://www.nmc-uk.org/Nurses-and-midwives/The-code/The-code-in-full/

Nozick, R. (1974) *Anarchy, State and Utopia.* Blackwell, Oxford.

Pearce, J.R., Richardson, E.A., Mitchell, R.J. & Shortt, N.K. (2010) *Environmental Justice and Health: The Implications of the Socio-Spatial Distribution of Multiple Environmental Deprivation for Health Inequalities in the United Kingdom.* Transactions of the Institute of British Geographers, 35 (4), 522–539 http://dx.doi.org/10.1111/j.1475-5661.2010.00399.x

Race Relations Act 1976 http://www.legislation.gov.uk/ukpga/1976/74 (Accessed 7 December 2010).

Rayner, C. & Hoel, H. (1997) A summary review of literature relating to workplace bullying. *Journal of Community and Applied Social Psychology,* 7, 181–191.

Rawls, J. (1999) *A Theory of Justice* (revised ed.). Oxford University Press, Oxford.

Smith, P.A., Allan, H.T., Henry, L., Larsen, J.A. & Mackintosh, M.M. (2006) Valuing and recognising the talents of a diverse healthcare workforce http://portal.surrey.ac.uk/portal/page?_pageid=886,928925&_dad=portal&_schema=PORTAL

Statutory Instrument (2003) *No. 1626 The Race Relations Act 1976 (Amendment) Regulations* 2003. Crown Copyright, London.

Templeton, S-K. (2009) *Lesbian couple win fight for IVF on the NHS* http://www.timesonline.co.uk/tol/life_and_style/health/article6719152.ece (Accessed 7 December 2010).

The Stephen Lawrence Inquiry Report of an Inquiry by Sir William Macpherson of Cluny http://www.archive.official-documents.co.uk/document/cm42/4262/4262.htm (Accessed 1 December2010).

Von Hippell, W. (2007) Brain atrophy in elderly leads to unintended racism, depression and problem gambling http://www.psychologicalscience.org/index.php/news/releases/brain-atrophy-in-elderly-leads-to-unintended-racism-depression-and-problem-gambling.html (Accessed 20 May 2011).

Waterfield, R. (1984) *Plato, Republic.* translation. Oxford University Press, Oxford.

Wolpert, S. (2008) Brain reacts to fairness as it does to money and choclate, study shows http://newsroom.ucla.edu/portal/ucla/brain-reacts-to-fairness-as-it-49042.aspx (Accessed 14 July 2010).

Chapter 8

Responding to unprofessional practice

Anna Brown

You may have heard it said that the United Kingdom (UK) National Health Service is the envy of the world. Patient rights and privileges as set out in the NHS Constitution (NHS 2010) include: free and accessible services; to have health needs assessed and responded to; and not to be unlawfully discriminated against in the provision of services. Most patients have a good journey through NHS and other health services, however, not all do and this can be due to individual and organisational failures. A report from the Commonwealth Fund, for example, rated UK healthcare as seventh out of seven countries for patient-centred care (Davis et al. 2010).

In 2009 the case a nurse, Margaret Haywood, stimulated debate about appropriate and inappropriate responses to unprofessional practice. The media described her as an 'undercover nurse' as she covertly filmed elderly patients in hospital receiving poor care. Her recording later appeared in a BBC *Panorama* documentary reporting the neglected conditions of these patients. Haywood was, initially, struck off the professional register for breaching confidentiality. The striking off order was later replaced with a 12 month caution (http://www.nmc-uk.org).

Sadly, unprofessional misconduct is not uncommon nor is it something that health professionals can ignore. Abuse and neglect in healthcare have been described as 'systemic' by one author (Mandelstam 2011). To avoid engaging in unprofessional practice and to know how to respond effectively should you witness such practice you need to be familiar with the range of activities that might constitute unprofessional practice and with appropriate reporting processes. This chapter examines ethical, legal and professional aspects of practice that fall below accepted standards and which may be described as unprofessional, unethical or as poor or bad care. This covers a wide range of professional actions and omissions which, crucially, result in patients and others being harmed, neglected or feeling distressed and undignified. The chapter will also examine the relationship between raising concerns and whistleblowing.

The two scenarios presented here are from healthcare practice, The first, relating to a couple in a maternity unit, has been anonymised to preserve confidentiality. The second case has been published on the Health Professions Council web-site and is in the public domain. You are invited to reflect on consent issues and to consider responses that are ethical, legal and professional. Aspects of consent will then be explored and an analysis of the scenarios will follow later in the chapter.

As you read the scenarios we suggest you have two questions in mind:

▶ If you were the professional, what would you do?
▶ Why would you respond this way? Refer to relevant ethical, legal and professional concepts and arguments that could support your action.

Scenarios

Making a decision about a paramedic's conduct

You are a member of the Fitness to Practice Committee at the Health Professions Council. As a member of the panel you have to make a decision about a paramedic whose case comes before the committee. The evidence you are presented with states that the paramedic had argued with a patient's mother regarding whether or not the patient should be taken to hospital. The patient had had five seizures and the paramedic had informed the ambulance crew that they did not have to take the patient to hospital. He then obtained a signature from the patient to the effect that he was refusing treatment and transport to hospital. You are told that the patient lacked capacity. In another situation, the same paramedic had failed to respond appropriately to a patient who was critically ill. He had also failed to provide continuous monitoring of the patient and had returned to the ambulance with the life support equipment 'leaving the patient in a critical state'.

The options open to the Fitness to Practice panel if it finds misconduct are to: take no further action; strike the paramedic off the professional register; suspend him from the register for a limited period; require conditions of practice; deliver a caution.

Concerns about the behaviour of an experienced colleague

Mrs Lidiard has been admitted to the delivery suite in early labour with her husband. Both she and her husband have learning disabilities and this is their first baby. You are a newly qualified midwife working with an experienced midwife colleague, Helen, on a delivery suite at night. Neither you nor your colleague had met the couple before. You are aware that they are known to social services and that there has been a case conference regarding their unborn baby. The plan is for social services to be involved with planning the discharge of this woman with her baby. It has been agreed that the parents will require assessment and close supervision with ongoing support to care for their baby. Helen makes it clear to you, in private, that she does not approve of people with learning disabilities having babies.

Mrs Lidiard is contracting every 5–6 minutes. On examination it is found that she is not in established labour. The delivery suite is full and there are no free beds. Mrs Lidiard is extremely anxious and does not want to be separated from her husband. Mr Lidiard asks the midwife if they might wait at home. He says that they have been informed of signs of advancing labour and have been given contact details to inform the midwife and hospital. Helen tells the couple that, in most cases, this would be acceptable but she has reservations in their case. Mrs Lidiard becomes upset but Helen does not stop to comfort her. You consider Helen's response to be unhelpful.

We will return to the scenarios later in the chapter.

What Is Unprofessional Practice?

Professional practice can be defined as practising a profession with a protected title, being required to register on a professional register and being held to account for professional standards which are nationally recognised standards and set in law (Health professionals' council standards 2009). For the purposes of this text, professional practice occurs when professionals act in accord with professional values, codes and guidelines, and within the law. Unprofessional practice occurs when professionals do not act in accord with ethical, professional and legal requirements. Unprofessional practice relates to behaviour that does not befit professionals and compromises their fitness to practice. The Health Professions Council (2010) identifies six areas that may impair fitness to practise:

- **Misconduct** – examples would include failing to provide adequate patient care; self-administration of medication; having a sexual relationship with a patient; attending work under the influence of drugs or alcohol.

▶ **Lack of competence** – examples might include failure to keep appropriate records; lack of clinical knowledge and skills; failure to provide adequate care.

▶ **Conviction or caution for a criminal offence** – this could include drink driving offences; assault; accessing child pornography; possessing illegal drugs.

▶ **Physical or mental health** – a range of health issues could impair a professional's fitness to practice, for example, addiction, alcoholism, psychosis or severe depression.

▶ **Decision reached by** another health and social care regulator.

▶ **Being barred** from working with vulnerable adults or children under the vetting and barring schemes.

It should be remembered that unprofessional practice, particularly incompetent practice, may also make the health professional accountable for negligence. This is discussed in detail in Chapters 1 and 2.

Behaviour which occurs outside a work environment can also be considered unprofessional if it results in you bringing your profession into disrepute or your competence and character into question. Activities which can be considered unprofessional could include being drunk and disorderly and inappropriate use, or disclosing inappropriate information on social websites, such as Facebook (NMC 2011). It should also be said that there are behaviours that are unprofessional but may not be considered serious enough to warrant reporting, for example, talking over a patient, shrugging when asked a question by a relative or not responding to a patient because it is time for a lunch break or to go off duty. Such instances may not cause direct physical harm or compromise patient safety but they may contribute to a patient or other person feeling distressed, anxious or disregarded.

Patient safety is an important aspect of patient care. Unfortunately, it is sometimes compromised due to incompetence, miscommunication or error. Georgiou (2009) distinguishes between two main types of incident: clinical incidents with the direct involvement of a client or patient; and non-clinical incidents relating to hazards with an indirect impact on the well-being of patients, staff and members of the public. Incidents can be adverse, a serious untoward occurrence or a near miss. An *adverse incident* is generally defined as an event or circumstances that could have or did lead to actual or possible personal injury, harm or damage. This would include a person slipping on a wet floor, tripping over equipment or falling out of bed or down stairs. Georgiou (2009: 42) defines *a serious untoward incident (SUI)* as 'in general terms something out of the ordinary or unexpected, with the potential to cause serious harm'. An example might be the administration of medication through an intravenous infusion to the wrong patient with life-threatening consequences. A *near miss* is an unplanned event that did not result in injury, illness, or damage, but had the potential to do so. An example might be where a paramedic intervenes to prevent another health professional administering medication that the patient had already received but had not been recorded.

Most of the examples given here suggest that these incidents are often accidental rather than intentional, and often due to haste and lack of adherence to procedure. While some incidents that compromise patient safety may be described as 'unprofessional', not all can. What would be described as unprofessional, however, would be the non-reporting of such incidents resulting in further harm to patients. This would also present a missed opportunity in terms of professional learning and the avoidance of such incidents in future (Johnstone 2004).

Incident reporting should take place within 24 hrs by completing appropriate forms (for example, the IR1 and IR2) which should be available in all clinical areas. For adverse reporting an HS1 form is usually available, near misses should also be reported and reviewed for 'lessons to be learnt' and management of situations and procedures reviewed and updated. Georgiou (2009) also suggests that these forms should be completed to contain factual detail which does not indicate admission of liability or personal opinion.

The information should then be reviewed by a line manager ensuring that the confidentiality of persons involved is maintained. In midwifery, a supervisor of midwives is usually also involved in this review process if this involves maternity care and midwives. However, whichever profession is involved immediate action is normally taken to ensure that professionals involved are supported and the client's needs and safety are ensured. Perry (2010) suggests that when situations arise in which actions and practices are scrutinised, having the support of your professional body representative or a supervisor of midwives is paramount. This can help to ensure factual clarity through submission of a statement which may be the only action that follows a reported incident. The National Reporting and Learning Service (NRLS) manages a national safety reporting system on behalf of the NHS in England and Wales (http://www.nrls.npsa.nhs.uk). It is mandatory for the NHS to report 'serious patient safety incidents' to the Care Quality Commission (CQC); however, if these are reported to the NRLS they are then forwarded to the CQC. Readers might consider how the range of safety topics identified by the NRLS relate to their own practice (see http://www.nrls.npsa.nhs.uk).

There is much to learn from public reports of healthcare situations which have compromised patient safety and well-being, sometimes over several years. It is recommended that you read the report from the Bristol Royal Infirmary Inquiry which detailed deficits in the management of care of children receiving complex cardiac surgery between 1984 and 1995 (Kennedy 2001). The report states that between 30 and 35 children under one died, between 1991 and 1995, more than might have been expected at that time. The report provides a range of explanations including lack of insight, communication, leadership and teamwork and in terms of 'a club culture' and 'an imbalance of power' with too much control in the hands of a few individuals' (Report Synopsis, Section 8). There were almost 200 recommendations in the inquiry report relating to: prioritising the needs of children in healthcare; safety; the competence of healthcare staff; the organisation and equitable treatment of healthcare staff; the development of agreed standards of care; and the need for openness and monitoring so that clinical performance can be evaluated and deficits identified (see http://www.bristol-inquiry.org.uk).

At the time of writing, the Mid Staffordshire NHS Foundation Trust Public Inquiry was in progress, chaired by Robert Frances QC (http://www.midstaffspublicinquiry.com). The remit of the inquiry was described by Mr Frances in a BBC interview: 'Last year, in my first inquiry, I sat and listened to many stories of appalling care [...] As I did so, the question that went constantly through my mind was 'why did none of the organisations charged with the supervision and regulation of our hospital detect that something serious was going on and why was nothing done about it' (BBC News http://www.bbc.co.uk). The focus of the fifth inquiry is, therefore, to examine 'the commissioning, supervisory and regulatory organisations in relation to their monitoring role between January 2005 and March 2009. It will consider why the serious problems at the Trust were not identified and acted on sooner, and will identify important lessons to be learnt for the future of patient care' (http://www.midstaffspublicinquiry.com/).

This is the fifth inquiry into the higher than expected mortality rates at Stafford Hospital between 2005 and 2008. It has been estimated that 'at least 400 people may have died unnecessarily or prematurely' and the fundamental care needs of patients were not responded to (Brindle 2010). *The Guardian* journalist, David Brindle (2010) drew attention to the role of student health professionals. He asked:

> What of the student, arriving innocently in such an environment? For, among the unanswered questions about what happened in Mid Staffs is the role played, or not, by hundreds of student nurses, midwives and other health professionals who were on placement at Stafford General hospital during the years under review. Did they notice anything amiss? Did they attempt to blow the whistle? Did their tutors take any action? The short answer to all three questions seems to be that they did not ... (http://www.guardian.co.uk)

It is strongly recommended that you read the Frances report and other such reports to understand how things can go wrong with a view to avoiding such errors and oversights. An important question that all of us need to consider, whether we are family members visiting patients, health professionals or students is: what would we do if we observed patient neglect? As will be discussed later, non-action is not an option. Chapter 2 made it clear that health professionals are responsible for their actions *and* their omissions. What becomes clear from such reports is that unsafe and unprofessional practice needs to be understood in relation to the behaviours and role of individuals and teams and within the context of complex organisations.

The ethical, professional and legal rationale for the promotion of good healthcare practice and the avoidance of unsafe and unprofessional practice has been described in Chapter 1 and examined throughout this text.

Ethical aspects

The four principles approach (Beauchamp & Childress 2009) to professional ethics directs professionals to: do good (beneficence); avoid harm (non-maleficence); provide patients with information and respect their decisions (respect for autonomy); and to treat people fairly by allocating benefits and burdens justly and not discriminating on unethical grounds (justice). In relation to understanding and responding to unprofessional practice a virtue-based approach is also helpful: health professionals need to reflect on their capacity for compassion and care in their practice and on their dispositions to support behaviours that demonstrate honesty and integrity. To raise concerns may, as discussed later, also require courage and professional wisdom (Banks & Gallagher 2009).

Legal aspects

All employers and employees have duties under the *Health and Safety at Work etc Act 1974* ss. 2–8 to ensure the health and safety of staff, clients/patients and any others affected by work practices. Breach of such duties can lead to disciplinary action by employers and even prosecution in the criminal courts. Additionally there may be liability under the civil law of negligence.

Professionals are sometimes concerned that they will suffer victimisation if they raise concerns. Protection against victimisation is enshrined in the *Public Interest Disclosure Act 1998*, also known as the Whistle Blowers Act. A professional who makes a *'qualifying disclosure'* which may include allegations of criminal offences by or against staff and clients, professionals failing to carry out their professional duties, a miscarriage of justice has occurred, or the health and safety of staff and patients is at risk is protected from dismissal or detriment resulting from the disclosure (*Employment Rights Act 1996* ss. 43A–43K inserted by the *Public Interest Disclosure Act 1998*).

Professional aspects

Both professional codes (Nursing and Midwifery Council 2008, Health Professions Council 2008) emphasise that health professionals must act in the best interests of patients and maintain high standards of practice at all times. Both the NMC and the HPC suggest that *'turning a blind eye'* or failing to take steps to deal with unsafe or unprofessional behaviour could be regarded as sufficiently serious to put the professional's registration at risk. Documents from both the NMC and HPC on *Raising and escalating concerns* in 2010 make it clear that non-action is not an option. You need to read this document carefully so you know what is required should you have concerns about standards of practice. The link to the NMC and HPC documents is on the reference list.

Reporting Incidents and Unprofessional Behaviour

Despite the fact that professionals now have clearly defined obligations to report incidents and unprofessional behaviour, there is evidence that this is not always easy. Research conducted by Firth-Cousins et al. (2003) suggested that nurses and doctors may not report for a range of reasons, for example: because the bad practice seems impossible to prove; they feared retribution; they didn't want to cause trouble; in the belief that they wouldn't have been listened to; due to lack of support; not wishing to hurt a colleague; not wanting to 'tell tales'; having no-one to talk to; due to being advised against reporting by peers; fear of financial loss. There is evidence that reporting unprofessional practice and in particular, whistleblowing (discussed below), is bad for people's health and well-being. However, not raising concerns is not an option for health professionals.

Pugh (2009) developed a substantive theory to explain how nurses deal with allegations of unprofessional behaviour. The author reiterates that the resultant harm to patients from breaching or failing to meet established standards of care in nursing and midwifery, is viewed as unprofessional conduct within a legislative framework. His theory suggests that when health professionals experience varying degrees of personal and professional vulnerability through being reported to regulatory authorities for alleged unprofessional behaviour, they are transformed personally and professionally. This can have an impact on psychosocial and professional issues which has identified a need to develop a framework for self- and external support. The findings of this study have implications for clinical management, education and research practices in nursing and midwifery.

Bence explored recent developments in reporting poor practice and reiterates the need for support to enable health professionals to report unprofessional behaviour and malpractice (RCN 2009b). Many health professionals are reluctant to disclose such behaviour, although professionals are bound by the Code of Conduct (NMC 2008). Gallagher (2010) suggests that insights from research may help professionals develop strategies to raise concerns as both a matter of professional and ethical obligations. They must seek support from their own professional bodies, organisational reporting frameworks and other external sources such as the National Patient Safety Agency and Public Concern at Work.

Dimond (2001) suggests several barriers to reporting incidents and lack of understanding of how to report incidence may be one reason. Georgiou (2009: 43) suggests that 'the point of clinical incident reporting is not to be punitive but to understand what has gone wrong'. A process through which such investigations can be carried out and addressed is suggested. However, those professionals taking such action must be aware that the more serious clinical incidents could result in disciplinary action through professional bodies such as the NMC and the HPC.

Raising Concerns about Unprofessional Practice v. Whistleblowing

The NMC (2010a: 7) distinguishes between 'raising and escalating a concern' and 'making a complaint'. *Raising a concern* means that the professional is worried about an issue, wrongdoing or risk which affects others. The professional has observed, been witness or when risks have been reported and steps are taken to draw attention to incidents or situations affecting patients, staff or the organisation. On the other hand, *making a complaint* involves reporting or pursuing a grievance procedure to an employer about personal treatment and the professional is seeking resolution.

Dougherty (1995: 2552) explains that whistleblowing 'refers to a warning issued by a member or former member of an organization to the public about a serious wrongdoing or danger created or concealed within the organization'.

Sellin (1995) defines the differences between whistleblowing from reporting when health professionals act as patient advocates within organisations. In Sellin's study, participants tended to view whistleblowing as an external action to an unresponsive organisation and reporting 'more as an internal process, done through organizational channels' (p. 23).

Fletcher et al. (1998) believe that cases of whistle blowing are indicative of an ethical failure at organisational level. The authors provide an analysis of whistleblowing in healthcare organisations and conclude that there is a need to refine approaches to organisational ethics and to protect staff who speak out in defence of patient health and welfare. Health professionals are ethically responsible for reporting unprofessional behaviour and the authors believe that whistle blowing is a moral action and necessary to protect the public Hunt (1995a). Wilmot (2000:1051) suggests that 'the ethics of whistleblowing can only be understood in relation to its moral purpose whether this is to achieve a good outcome (a consequentialist view) or fulfil a duty [of care to the client or to the employer] (a deontological view)'.

A health professional may be torn between personal value judgements and loyalty to an employer when considering reporting unprofessional practice Hunt (1995b). There may be the additional fear of losing one's job and incurring personal financial hardship. However, Silva and Synder (1992) suggest that disloyalty to an organisation implies that mutual respect and confidentiality are breached making this dilemma more difficult.

It is unclear how well informed most professionals are about whistleblowing and the implications of taking such action. Public Concern at Work (PCaW 2008) published a survey on whistle blowing which indicated that nurses are more willing to raise concerns especially where Trusts safeguard the interests of their staff. They may be supported and encouraged by their employing a Trust to bring to light concerns about practice for the benefit and protection of clients and patients. A blame free culture will ensure that concerns are highlighted and addressed but staff must be aware of due processes through which such issues are managed. More recently the Royal College of Nursing (RCN) (2009a) reported findings of a survey on whistleblowing by nurses which suggests that 78 per cent feared negative consequences if reporting concerns to employers and therefore only 46 per cent of those participants surveyed said they would be confident enough to report these concerns. Consequently the RCN has launched a phone line to support whistleblowers.

Whistleblowers are morally justified in their actions if ethical principles have been considered and advocacy to the client supersedes the nurse's or midwife's own loyalties. Health professionals must ensure that they have also considered issues of responsibility and accountability according to their Code of Professional Conduct (NMC 2008). However, professionals are faced with behaving ethically and the reality of their organisation when faced with reporting allegations of unprofessional practice. Hunt (1992) argues that organisations have an ethical responsibility to support staff who report poor practice. In addition, the member of staff being reported for unprofessional conduct must also be protected. McDonald (2002) reported those affected by the whistleblowing act may also suffer an impact on their personal and professional life in terms of physical and emotional health.

The NMC (2010a) recommends that when raising a concern it should be done openly with professionals providing their name such that the concern can be investigated. Some professionals may choose to remain anonymous or their identity remains confidential but this makes addressing the matter more difficult. Legislation is in place to protect those who have genuine concerns and are acting in the public interest (*The Public Interest Disclosure Act 1998*).

How Should a Health Professional Report Unprofessional Practice?

It is important to establish that there are reasonable grounds to believe that the person being reported has breached professional standards. It is enough for the person making the allegation to act in good faith on the basis that the information is substantially true. Once this is established the concerns must be brought to the attention of the employer or person designated to deal with such issues. Once the allegation has been made, an employer will follow known procedures to bring the matter to a conclusion. This must include informing the alleged wrongdoer of the allegations and ensuring that they are given a full opportunity to present their own case.

Suspension from duty and enquiry through the NMC or HPC may follow. The appropriate committee will decide whether to maintain them on the register or remove them from further practice. It must always be remembered that the committee may find that no breach of professional standards has occurred. Readers are advised to read the Health Professions Council Fitness to Practise annual report (HPC 2010) as it details the process and cases heard in the 2009–2010 period. It may be of interest to the reader to attend Fitness to Practise hearings which are generally open to the public. These events provide many lessons from which professionals can learn. You can find details regarding how to book a place to observe a hearing on the HPC and NMC web-site.

The next section revisits the two scenarios introduced at the beginning of this chapter. The outcome of each will be described and the ethical, legal and professional issues that apply to each discussed.

Application to Scenarios

Making a decision about a paramedic's conduct

This was an actual case referred to the Fitness to Practise Committee at the Health Professions Council (HPC). The paramedic was struck off the HPC Register for 'failing to accurately treat patients, failing to inform second ambulance crews about the treatment of patients and behaving without compassion, feeling or tact towards a patient and his family while working with the Yorkshire ambulance service NHS Trust'. (See http://www.hpc-uk.org).

The purpose of the Fitness to Practise process is to protect the public from professionals who are not fit to practice due to deficits in skills, knowledge and character. How easy did you find it to make a judgement and what did you have in mind as you deliberated about the scenario?

Ethical issues

From the description of the paramedic's action it seems clear that he did not act in keeping with the principles of beneficence, non-maleficence and justice. He also, it seemed, asked a patient who lacked capacity to sign a form saying he did not wish to go to hospital. If you were a panel member you might well ask if, and how, the paramedic might have known that the patient lacked capacity. The information presented suggests also that the paramedic did not demonstrate care, compassion or sensitivity in his interaction with patients and families.

Legal issues

No specific legal issues arise save for the general requirement that the committee act in a way which is fair and that any punishment is proportionate. A decision can sometimes be challenged in the Courts by way of a process known as judicial review (see Chapter 7).

Professional issues

The sections of the HPC code (2008) that were violated appear to include: sections 1 (acting in best interests of patients); 3 (maintaining high standards of personal conduct); 7 (maintain proper and effective communication with patients and others); 13 (carry out your duties in a professional and ethical way); and 14 (behave with honesty and integrity).

Concerns about the behaviour of an experienced colleague

The newly qualified midwife was concerned about the response of her experienced colleague, Helen, towards Mr and Mrs Lidiard. She had reason to believe that Helen was discriminating against the couple based on their learning disabilities. The newly qualified midwife believed that encouraging the couple to stay in hospital was appropriate but that

Helen's treatment of them was unhelpful. She discussed the case with her line manager who re-assured her that a discussion with Helen would take place.

Ethical issues

The description of Helen's behaviour suggests that although she may have justified her decision on the basis of patient safety, however, the couple may have been distressed or harmed emotionally by her intervention. She did not appear to engage the couple in a discussion regarding the best course of action and the reasons for recommending they remain in hospital. Her action could be described as paternalistic (See discussion of paternalism in Chapter 5). A professional's decision to support a patient's autonomy could, of course, be in direct conflict with his or her professional wisdom in making sound decisions and swayed by wishes, values and beliefs (Foster and Lasser 2010). Axten (2003) suggests that professionals may believe that what they do is for the good of the patient with sometimes little awareness that the decisions taken may be for their own as well as the patient's benefit. This makes the patient dependant on the professional and although seeming to be handling the power of decision making to the client, the professional remains in control.

Legal issues

The health professional is required to act competently. This obviously covers the actual treatment decisions made but it also means that the professional must have full regard to the need for commitment to equality and diversity. In this scenario it appears that the more experienced colleague may discriminate against those with learning disability. She would also appear to be unaware of the legislation regarding mental capacity and the need to ensure all efforts are made to assist a patient's understanding (*Mental Capacity Act 2005* s.1(3)).

You will recollect from your reading of Chapter 2 that all professionals are accountable for their own practice. There may be liability for negligence if the professional has failed to act competently with the result that the patient has suffered injury. In this scenario it would appear that no injury has been caused. This does not mean, however, that there is no possibility of legal liability. The *Equality Act 2010* s.6 makes it clear that discrimination on the ground of disability is unlawful.

The issue of capacity to make an autonomous decision is also relevant. You will remember that under the *Mental Capacity Act 2005* s.1(2) everyone is to be treated as having capacity unless the contrary is proved. Section 3(2) makes it clear that all appropriate means, for example, '*simple language, visual aids or any other means*, should be used to assist the patient's ability to understand what is happening and what decisions need to be made. It seems that the more experienced midwife has assumed a lack of capacity simply by reason of the fact that the patient has learning disability.

Professional issues

The midwife should also have been aware of the need to share information with colleagues if she believed Mrs Lidiard may be at risk of harm from the discriminatory attitude of the more experienced midwife. A trusting relationship between the patient and professional can be destroyed if an act of unprofessional behaviour, such as discrimination, is perceived by the patient. However, the patient with learning difficulties may not have been fully aware of the risks she faced and was limited in her ability to give consent. Therefore the law, ethical principles and The Code (2008) protects the public and a midwife, 'must share with people, in a way they can understand, the information they want or need to know about their health" and "must act as an advocate for those in her care'. It should be noted that midwives are also bound by the NMC's *Midwives Rules and Standards* (2010b). Midwives need to be familiar with this document.

There appears to have been a breakdown in communication regarding the management of Mr and Mrs Lidiard. The newly qualified midwife is also accountable for her actions and should, in view of her previous knowledge and history of the couple, perhaps have challenged her more experienced colleague (Curtis et al. 2006, Gould 2008).

Conclusion

This chapter has explored the topic of unprofessional practice in healthcare. Most patients who journey through our health services will have good experiences and reason to commend health professionals for their care and competence. However, as the scenarios and some of the discussion in this chapter have demonstrated, there is no room for complacency. When things do go wrong you need to learn from them and draw on this learning to prevent unprofessional practice in the future. You also need to get in the habit of learning from exemplary professionals who role model professional behaviour. You need to develop knowledge, skills and moral dispositions that enable you to respond appropriately when practice compromises the safety and well-being of patients and others.

The introduction referred to the case of Margaret Haywood, who covertly filmed unprofessional practice that was subsequently shown on a television documentary. Opinion was divided as to whether Haywood's action was harmful or not and whether or not she lacked wisdom in taking the course of action she did (Belshaw 2010; Wainwright 2010). In response to Haywood and other cases, the NMC and HPC published guidelines on raising and escalating concerns that should now help you to understand the appropriate process you need to follow. There would appear to be no good reason for health professionals to say, in future, that they did not know what to do should they observe bad practice. There is no need to be a bystander who permits unprofessional practice to continue nor to take action that may inadvertently harm patients or the reputation of your profession. The next chapter provides you with the opportunity to reflect more on the relationship between individual professionals and organisations in promoting professional practice.

References

Axten S. (2003) Power how it is used and sometimes abused *British Journal of Midwifery* 11 (11), 681–684.

Banks, S. & Gallagher, A. (2009) *Ethics in Professional Life: Virtues for Health and Social Care.* Palgrave Macmillan, Basingstoke.

BBC News, http://www.bbc.co.uk/news/health-11696735 Accessed 27 January 2011.

Beauchamp, T.L. & Childress, J.F. (2009) *Principles of Biomedical Ethics* (6th ed.). Oxford University Press, Oxford.

Belshaw, C. (2010) Response to Paul Wainwright's "Undercover nurse" struck off the professional register for misconduct. *Nursing Ethics,* 17(1), 133–134.

Brindle, D. (2010) Whistle-blowing cloud over students at scandal hospital. *The Guardian* 02/11/2010 (http://www.guardian.co.uk/education/2010/nov/02/students-hospital-scandal Accessed 30 May 2011).

Bristol Royal Infirmary Inquiry, http://www.bristol-inquiry.org.uk/final_report/report/ Summary2.htm Accessed 26 January 2011.

Curtis, P., Ball, L. & Kirkham, M. (2006) Working together? Indices of division within the midwifery workforce. *British Journal of Midwifery,* 14(3), 138–141.

Davis, K., Schoen, C. & Stremikis, K. (2010) *Mirror, Mirror on the Wall: How the U.S. Health Care System Compares Internationally.* Update Commonwealth Fund.

Dimond, B. (2001) The National Patient Safety Agency. *British Journal of Midwifery,* 9 (8), 511–514.

Dougherty, C.J. (1995) 'Whistleblowing in health care' in W.T. Reich (Ed. in Chief), *Encyclopedia of Bioethics* (Rev.ed.). Simon & Schuster Macmillan, New York.

Equality Act 2010. The Stationery Office, London.

Firth-Cozens, J., Firth, R.A. & Booth, S (2003) Attitudes to and experience of reporting poor care. *Clinical Governance: An International Journal,* 8(4), 331–336.

Foster, I.R. & Lasser, J. (2010) *Professional Ethics in Midwifery Practice.* Jones & Bartlett Publications, London.

Fletcher, J.J., Sorrell, J.M. & Cipriano Silva, M. (1998) Whistle blowing as a failure of organisational ethics. *The Online Journal of Issues in Nursing,* 3(3) Manuscript 3.

Frances, R. (2010) *Robert Frances Inquiry Report into Mid Staffordshire NHS Foundation Trust* Crown Copyright (see http://www.dh.gov.uk/en/Publicationsandstatistics/ Publications/PublicationsPolicyAndGuidance/DH_113018 accessed 30/05/2011)

Gallagher, A. (2010) Whistleblowing: what influences nurses' decisions on whether to report poor practice? *Nursing Times*, 106(4).

Georgiou, G. (2009) What do I do now? *Midwives* Dec/Jan, 42–43.

Gould, D. (2008) Professional dominance and subversion in maternity services. *British Journal of Midwifery*, 16(2), 210.

Health Professions Council Standards of Conduct Performance and Ethics 2008 (http://www.hpc-uk.org/publications/standards/index.asp?id=38)

Health Professions Council (2009) Standards (http://www.hpc-uk.org/aboutregistration/standards/ Accessed 30 May 2011).

Health Professions Council (2010) Fitness to Practise Annual Report http://www.hpc-uk.org/publications/reports/index.asp?id=403

Health Professional Council (2010) Raising and Escalating Concerns in the Workplace http://www.hpc-uk.org/registrants/raisingconcerns/ Accessed 28 January 2011.

Health Professions Council, http://www.hpc-uk.org/mediaandevents/pressreleases/index.asp?id=457 Accessed 22 January 2011

Health & Safety at Work Act (1974) (c37) The Stationery Office, London.

Hollis-Martin, C.J. & Bull, P. (2008) Obedience and conformity in clinical practice. *British Journal of Midwifery*, 16(8), 504–509.

Hunt, G. (1992) News Focus. *Nursing Times*, 88(25), 1–22.

Hunt, G. (1995a) 'Conclusion: A new accountability?' in G. Hunt (Ed.), *Whistleblowing in the Health Service: Accountability, Law and Professional Practice*. Edward Arnold, London, pp. 155–158.

Hunt, G. (1995b) 'Introduction: Whistleblowing and the breakdown of accountability' in Hunt, G. (Ed.), *Whistleblowing in the Health Service: Accountability, Law and Professional Practice* (xvii), Edward Arnold, London.

Johnstone, M.J. (2004) Patient safety, ethics and whistleblowing. *Australian health Review,* 28 (1), 13–19.

Kennedy, I. (2001) *The Bristol Royal Infirmary Inquiry Final Report* http://www.bristol-inquiry.org.uk/final_report/report/index.htm Accessed 29 January 2011.

Mandelstam M. (2011) *How We Treat the Sick: Neglect and Abuse in our Health Services*. Jessica Kingsley Publishers, London.

Mental Capacity Act 2005. The Stationery Office, London.

McDonald, S. (2002) Physical and emotional effects of whistleblowing. *Journal of Psychosocial and Mental Health,* 40, 14–27.

Mid Staffordshire NHS Foundation Trust, http://www.midstaffspublicinquiry.com/news/2011/05/thursday-26-may-2011-transcript Accessed 30 May 2011.

National Reporting and Learning Service (NRLS), http://www.nrls.npsa.nhs.uk/reporta-patient-safety-incident/about-reporting-patient-safety-incidents/ http://www.nrls.npsa.nhs.uk/resources/patient-safety-topics/ Both accessed 30 May 2011.

NHS (2010) The NHS Constitution: The NHS Belongs to Us All http://www.nhs.uk/choiceintheNHS/Rightsandpledges/NHSConstitution/Documents/nhs-constitution-interactive-version-march-2010.pdf (Accessed 29 January 2011).

NMC (2008) *The Code: Standards of Conduct, performance and ethics for nurses and midwives* (http://www.nmc-uk.org/Nurses-and-midwives/The-code/The-code-in-full/ Accessed 30 May 2011).

Nursing and Midwifery Council (2010a) Raising and escalating concerns http://www.nmc-uk.org/Nurses-and-midwives/Raising-and-escalating-concerns/ (Accessed 20 January 2011).

Nursing and Midwifery Council (2010b) *Midwives Rules and Standards* NMC, London.

Nursing and Midwifery Council, http://www.nmc-uk.org/Press-and-media/News-archive/Joint-NMC-and-RCN-statement-on-Margaret-Haywood-High-Court-verdict/, accessed 30 May 2011.

NMC (2011) Social Networking Sites (published 1 July 2011).

Perry, N. (2010) Somebody to lean on. *Midwives: RCM Journal,* Dec, 24–25.

Public Concern at Work- www. Pcaw.co.uk

Public Interest Disclosure Act (1998),

Pugh, D. (2009) The Phoenix process: a substantive theory about allegations of unprofessional conduct. *Journal of Advanced Nursing,* 65(10), 2027–2037.

Royal College of Nursing (2009a) *RCN Launches Phone Line to Support Whistleblowing Nurses.* RCN tinyurl.com/phone-whistle, London.

Royal College of Nursing (2009b) *Defending Dignity: Challenges and Opportunities for Nursing.* RCN, London.

Sellin, S.C. (1995) Out on a limb: A qualitative study of patient advocacy in institutional nursing. *Nursing Ethics: An International Journal for Health professionals, 2*(1), 19–29.

Silva, M.C. & Synder, P. (1992) The ethics of whistleblowing by nurses, *Nursing Connections* 5(3), 17–21.

Wainwright, P. (2010) Reply (to Belshaw re "undercover nurse"). *Nursing Ethics,* 17(1), 135–136.

Wilmot, S. (2000) Nurses and whistleblowing: the ethical issues. *Journal of Advanced Nursing,* 32(5), 1051–1057.

Chapter 9

Promoting professional
healthcare practice

Jane Leng and Deborah Macartney

Healthcare is the subject of considerable and legitimate scrutiny. The media, for example, regularly report on healthcare deficits due to organisational failure or professional incompetence and negligence. Such reports challenge the professional image of professionals and may result in a loss of public trust and confidence. Professional healthcare practice is complex and takes place in an ever-changing environment. An awareness and understanding of the ethical, professional and legal aspects of care, as discussed in previous chapters, will help you to deliver a quality service.

It is important that you behave professionally, gaining public confidence and reassuring individuals that the health professions are patient- focused, competent and safe. Legally you have a duty to promote the well-being of clients by ensuring that you are a competent professional and must recognise the limitations of your scope of practice. Further, as a health professional you are bound by a code of conduct and are accountable– ethically, legally and professionally – for your own practice (See Chapter 2). You need, therefore, to be able to articulate the rationale for your actions and your omissions.

Professional and ethical healthcare practice is, of course, much less newsworthy than bad practice and questions regarding what makes this possible and sustainable are too rarely asked. To be a health professional is to have multiple demands made on your standards of behaviour that go beyond those that might be expected in other contexts. Upholding such standards in situations where there are competing priorities and perspectives can be demanding: your own values, for example, may clash with those of other team members; you may fear that the cost of speaking out against what you think is wrong is too high; or you may experience divided loyalties. It will not always be enough to know what the right thing to do is. You must also have the skills and courage to be able to apply such knowledge in your every-day professional practice.

This chapter explores the meaning of professional healthcare practice and highlights the potential for both individuals and organisations to enhance care through decision making within a legal and ethical framework. It examines the barriers that may be encountered in the delivery of high standards of care and discusses the qualities of people and environments which have been identified as critical in the facilitation of professional healthcare. Underpinning such discussion will be consideration of the need to understand individual actions in the context of the groups and institutions in which those actions take place.

We begin with two scenarios that invite you to reflect on consent issues and to consider responses that are ethical, legal and professional. Aspects of consent will then be explored and an analysis of the scenarios will follow later in the chapter.

As you read the scenarios we suggest that you have two questions in mind:

- If you were the professional, what would you do?
- Why would you respond this way? Refer to relevant ethical, legal and professional concepts and arguments that could support your action.

Scenarios

The missing clamp

It was a very hot summer's day in the operating theatres and the air conditioning was not working efficiently. This was the third consecutive case and staff were trying to stay cool. The situation had been reported. The male patient was in theatre to have abdominal surgery. He was obese and also had diabetes. The operation proceeded well and during the final stages of the procedure the swab and instrument count was performed. As the first layer was being closed all swabs and instruments were counted. At the skin layer, another count was performed and it was noted and appropriately reported to the surgeon that there was a 9' Spencer Wells clamp missing. This had been used to secure the muscle and fat layers during surgery. The surgeon dismissed the fact and was then called away to a trauma, leaving his senior registrar to complete the surgery.

You are a newly qualified operating department professional. You are concerned that a clamp is missing, however, other members of the theatre team seem prepared to continue the procedure without any further discussion.

Futile care?

Gemma is five years old and has been diagnosed with a high grade neuroblastoma. This is a neuroendocrine malignant tumour which often originates in the adrenal glands but can also affect nerve tissue in the neck, chest , abdomen and pelvis. The diagnosis followed a history of tiredness, loss of appetite and pain in her legs eighteen months ago. By the time the tumour was diagnosed it had spread from Gemma's adrenal glands to her liver. She underwent surgery followed by a long course of chemotherapy and radiotherapy which was upsetting for her but her condition did then stabilise. Gemma became very unwell while visiting her grandparents 100 miles from her home and is now complaining of difficulty swallowing as well as shortness of breath. She has a fever, is very drowsy and moaning in pain. Gemma's mother, who is most distressed, has taken her to the local Accident and Emergency Department from where the child is admitted to the hospital's paediatric High Dependency Unit.

Gemma is seen by the medical registrar who diagnoses continued spread of the cancer to her neck and pneumonia. He prescribes new chemotherapy, physiotherapy and antibiotics. In addition he recommends creation of a Percutaneous Endoscopic Gastrostomy (PEG) for feeding purposes and the commencement of ventilatory support should her respirations deteriorate. Gemma's mother states 'If that is what you think is best'.

You are the admitting nurse and try to comfort Gemma and her mother. You are concerned that the current treatment plan is futile and believe that it would be more appropriate to have palliative care. You feel torn. You are very uncomfortable at the prospect of being left with Gemma and her mother delivering care you do not agree with.

Understanding Professional Practice

Discussion in previous chapters has focused on the application of ethical principles, rules and concepts to practice situations. For the most part, the discussion has been concerned with the actions and omissions of a health professional. As professionals are individually accountable this is at is should be; however, it is also helpful to understand the individual and organisational barriers to, and enablers of, ethical practice. Two new concepts are introduced in this chapter that should help you to understand these processes: *moral distress*; and *ethical climate*.

Moral Distress

In both of the above scenarios you may be clear about the 'right' thing to do but in reality you may feel inhibited from enacting those decisions given the responses of those around you. Jameton (1984, 1993) used the term 'moral distress' to describe the painful feelings of an individual who has made a decision about a particular situation but is constrained from carrying out that decision, for example, by co workers and the institutional context of care. He distinguished this concept from that of moral dilemma when a decision is yet to be made between two or more ethical principles. Jameton (1993) further described two forms of moral distress: 'initial distress' refers to the anger and anxiety felt when confronted by obstacles and conflict with others' values; and 'reactive distress' to the uneasiness felt by people when they do not act upon their initial distress.

The prolongation of life through aggressive treatment is a situation that has often been described as generating moral distress (Corley 2002; Redman & Fry 2000; Wilkinson 1987/8.) Indeed, much of the research on moral distress has identified it as a phenomenon associated with acute and specialised areas of nursing (Austin et al. 2009; Elpern 2005; Gutierrez 2005; Lutzen et al. 2010.) However, as Hamric (2000) comments, most nurses will recognise this concept from their own practice and indeed it may affect all categories of health professional (Kalvemark et al. 2003).

It is also important to note that moral distress can be specific to a particular context and person (Pijl-Zeiber et al. 2008.) The same situation can cause moral distress in one person and not another. Wilkinson (1987/8), for example, identified that, in responding to a cardiac arrest, some nurses would suffer moral distress if resuscitation was done while others would suffer similar distress if resuscitation was not done, depending on their own values. Equally, health professionals with a high degree of moral sensitivity may experience greater degrees of moral distress than less sensitive professionals (Lutzen et al. 2010).

A range of factors have been identified as increasing the likelihood of the development of moral distress, one of which is staffing shortages (Corley et al. 2005; Zuzelo 2007.) Such shortages may contribute to moral distress by limiting the potential for effective communication within the multidisciplinary team as well as the opportunity for staff to get to know clients and increase difficulties for staff in the prioritisation of care (Austin et al. 2003; Hamric 2000).

Wilkinson (1987/8) notes that a health professional is most likely to experience moral distress in those circumstances where his or her values are different from that of other health professionals working in environment and the institution itself. First, there may be a conflict between organisational priorities in the effective management of limited resources and personal as well as professional ethics such as putting the patient first (Holly 1993). Institutional policies, for example, may limit access to the most effective wound dressings and pressure relieving devices. Silva et al. (2008) argue that such conflicts are greater if resource allocation processes are not open and transparent. Similarly professional relationships characterised by conflict in values and hierarchy can, as illustrated by Kalevemark et al. (2003) and Scenario 2, contribute to moral distress.

A further potent source of moral distress is associated with advocacy. Sundin-Huard and Fahry (1999) describe the distress of nurses who challenge medical treatment deemed to be inappropriate but are unsuccessful in that advocacy. Erlen (2001) further describes the institutional barriers there may be to advocacy such as power imbalance, a tradition of deference and a lack of self-esteem.

Such a sense of powerlessness may be exacerbated by lack of support within an organisation. Redman and Fry (2000) highlighted that many nurses who were in dispute with doctors about patient care found their organisation disinclined to address the issues and nurses did not perceive that they had anywhere to take their concerns so the conflict remained unresolved.

Moral distress may be under-recognised but there is substantial evidence of its deleterious effects: health professionals may experience a profound sense of failure and loss of integrity if they are not able to act in accordance with moral decisions (Kelly 1998.) Wilkinson (1987/8) describes the pervasive impact that moral distress may have on an individual's personal life and how it can lead to physical symptoms, such as heart palpitations and headaches, as well as mental anguish, anxiety and depression. In addition, moral distress may affect patient care. It has been associated with reduced communication within the healthcare team and withdrawal from patients (Gutierrez 2005).) Austin (2003) highlights how it may also diminish the capacity to deliver high quality care. Moral distress has, further, been linked to poor job satisfaction and burnout (Nathaniel 2002.) A number of studies identify moral distress as a factor in nurses' resignations and decisions to leave the profession (Corley 2002).

It is, therefore, argued that greater attention should be given to the concept of moral distress so that health professionals are better prepared for the challenges they may face in practice and emphasis should be given to creation of a climate where moral distress is minimised.

Ethical Climate

An 'ethical climate' relates to shared perceptions of organisational practices in relation to ethical decision making and reflection (Olson 1995). The issues of power, trust and human interaction within an organisation are raised within this concept and so it is possible to see the relevance of understanding the ethical climate within which you work in order to promote professional practice.

In her research on ethical climate, Olson (1995) found that nurses were more likely to report incompetence in practice than they were to report actual mistakes in the healthcare environment. Olsen's work linked the significance of ethical climate to decision making in that a positive climate encourages an open atmosphere of mutual respect and dialogue in what is right and wrong for patient care.

Good professional teamwork is vital within healthcare regardless of the setting, to ensure accurate transfer of information, effective decision making and appropriate patient management. This approach creates a positive ethical climate for the professional to work in order to provide safe and competent care. Professional accountability means we are accountable to our profession which in turn means we are judged according to professional standards. If a concern has been reported our professional regulatory bodies will make a judgement on whether a professional is fit to practice. Open communication can encourage trust and effective human interaction which is necessary to ensure a good standard of practice thereby supporting each individual and preventing a sense of isolation for the professional. Poor communication is almost always a fact in healthcare error so effective communication will support a more patient-focused approach to care (Dlugacz 2010). As an accountable professional the ethical climate can provide a nurturing environment in which to flourish and grow into a competent professional.

By improving the ethical climate there is a good probability that the ethical stress faced by a professional will be reduced. If nurses encounter moral distress in their position then there is likelihood that they will consider leaving either the position or indeed the profession.

Moreover, if a professional has a sense of disempowerment it could result in the delivery of poor patient care. Therefore by creating a positive ethical climate you as a professional can feel supported and hopefully as a result gain job satisfaction. This in itself starts to promote professional practice.

Application to Scenarios

The missing clamp

In Scenario 1, the patient was transferred to the recovery suite. His condition deteriorated rapidly and he had symptoms of shock. This was detected by a nurse recording his vital signs and who reported a dramatic drop in blood pressure. An emergency situation developed and the patient was immediately returned to theatre when it was discovered that the clamp had been left *in situ*.

The incident was formally reported and an investigation undertaken. The team met to debrief and discuss the incident in detail. The clamp had flipped underneath the peritoneum, as it was attached to the end to give a straight suture line and the surgeon had overlooked it. The surgeon later said that he had struggled to retract the patient's fat layers and in the heat of the theatre had rushed the suturing.

The operating department professional admitted that he had lacked the confidence to challenge the surgeon's decision to continue with the suturing. This was due to limited clinical experience and also the fear of being labelled by new colleagues as a trouble maker. A preceptor was allocated to him for a six month period to offer support and guidance.

The patient was informed of the incident and appeared to accept the situation without any indication of intent to complain. The patient recovered fully and was discharged home with a community team care package.

In this case no individual professional was held fully accountable for the incident. It was accepted that an accumulation of both system and human factors lead to the outcome. Team activity and theatre protocols were reviewed and an open culture encouraged to promote collaboration in professional practice. The air conditioning system was repaired within two days.

Ethical issues

To understand the events which took place in the theatre setting it is important to consider the human and system factors involved (Reason 2008) . These factors impact on team dynamics, affect patient outcomes and can raise legal and ethical concerns. Although the safety of the count checking procedure was in place the workforce pressure on the surgeon had a significant impact on team interaction. Decision making was affected and junior colleagues felt disempowered to contribute due to their apparent lack of experience when faced with the seniority of the surgeon.

So combined the systems factor of a faulty air conditioning system and the workforce pressure on the surgeon affected the human factor of decision making. Reason (2008) explains the significance of both human and systems factors where systems are the organisation's, or work settings and conditions which staff are faced with in their everyday practice. Therefore if we take this a step further and say that by understanding the interaction between a professional and the environment in order to prevent harm to our patients, we are promoting professional practice and creating a positive ethical climate in which to work.

Legal issues

The law demands a reasonable standard of care and behaviour from you as a professional (Griffith & Tengnah 2010). Both professional awareness and clinical competence will develop with experience; however, you are at all times accountable for your actions. Health professionals, including students, will not generally be able to argue that they are unaccountable because of a lack of experience The issue of clinical competence extends to all health professionals regardless of their status or stage of development. This issue is discussed in more detail in Chapters 1 and 2. If we consider the actions of each individual in Scenario 1, negligence needs to be considered with regards to poor, incompetent or inappropriate practice which caused a person harm or injury. Clearly the surgeon is accountable to the General Medical Council. This book is not intended to address medical practice but in discussing professional behaviour and decision making in this context the surgeon's activity is relevant in developing our understanding of legal and ethical issues. If the patient pursued a claim for compensation it might be possible to prove that the risk assessment necessary before undertaking the final stage of suturing was not adhered to, thereby compromising this particular patient's safety. The patient would appear to have a valid claim for damages on the basis of injury caused by the breach of duty, that is a failure to act competently in the circumstances.

Professional issues

According to Thompson and Dowding (2002) health professionals need to have a good understanding of the judgements and decisions they make in practice as accountable professionals. Therefore ethical decision making requires professionals to be fair and just in their approach to patient care which in turn may reduce stress-related decisions experienced by a professional. However, concerning evidence emerged from research conducted by Pauly et al. (2009) whereby it was found that nurses find it difficult to enact their professional and ethical values in the current healthcare environment.

We have a responsibility to support colleagues in practice, whether this be as a mentor, supervisor or manager. In this scenario there are three examples of junior staff needing support by more senior colleagues. First, the newly appointed scrub nurse needed support in his concerns about the missing clamp. The checking procedure was in place for the purpose of safety and it required all team members to participate especially when concern was raised. Second the Registrar was left to complete a task requiring skill and experience. He had a responsibility to respond to the ODP's concern before the final suturing process, but as a junior surgeon it may not have been acceptable to challenge senior colleagues. It may also have been the case that the pressure to complete the task successfully affected the ability to collaborate with colleagues.

Members of the professional healthcare team should present as good role models and offer support mechanisms for less experienced colleagues. In Scenario 1 above, the professionals working with the junior staff had a responsibility to guide and direct in a situation whereby decision making was dependent on experience. Professional practice depends on effective interaction and communication which in turn should improve a patient's experience of the healthcare system.

When considering patient involvement in their care and our part as professionals in that collaboration, it is worth noting that the National Patient Safety Agency (NPSA) re-launched Being Open (NPSA 2009) to encourage healthcare teams to be honest with patients and carers. Open and honest communication with patients is at the heart of healthcare. Research has shown that being open when things go wrong can help patients and staff to cope better with the after effects of a patient safety incident.

Understandably truth telling can present professionals with concern, especially if they have been directly involved in the event that has taken place. However, to engage the patient in a holistic manner shows a respect both for their human rights and autonomy in the decision-making process. The new framework is a best practice guide for all healthcare staff and it explains the principles behind *Being Open* outlining how to communicate with patients, their families and carers following harm.

Futile care?

The nurse in question was able to ask the doctor to delay commencement of the treatment plan until there had been an opportunity to discuss the situation further with Gemma's mother. In addition she ensured that Gemma had adequate pain relief. The nurse then spoke to Gemma's mother who told her that she did not want Gemma to suffer any longer and that Gemma herself had told her that she did not want any further treatment and that she just wanted to be at home. The nurse was then able to mediate between the family and doctor to revise the treatment plan. The next day Gemma was discharged home having been referred to the local community paediatric community palliative care team. She died peacefully two weeks later.

Ethical issues

The decision-making process in relation to the care of children with life limiting conditions can be fraught with emotion and call into question fundamental values. If the nurse was to be an effective patient and family advocate in this situation she would have needed to understand and manage the complexities underpinning different people's responses and be confident in her own capacity to employ ethical principles in order to secure quality care (Jacobs 2005).

The proposed treatment for Gemma had been described as 'futile' but the meaning of this term is contested. A distinction has been made between physiological and qualitative futility (Mohammed & Peter 2009.) Physiological futility refers to treatment which is unable to lead to a defined medical outcome. Qualitative futility, however, is associated with treatment which involves a burden that does not justify its benefits.

In reaching decisions about Gemma's care it was therefore important to be clear about the goals of treatment and a judgement had to be made about the benefits of an intervention in comparison to the burden of that treatment (Stark et al. 2008). The doctor might have considered that the new chemotherapy regime could have made a difference both to Gemma's symptoms and prognosis and was therefore worth trying. Antibiotics could also have eased Gemma's breathing and therefore promoted comfort. The nurse may, however, have been concerned that chemotherapy could have had unpleasant side-effects without having the prospect of changing the outlook for Gemma and that, although antibiotics may have extended Gemma's life, it would have meant that she would only live to endure further suffering. The doctor might also have thought that it would help Gemma's mother to see that everything that could be done had been done.

The nurse's primary concern may have been non-maleficence, to do the patient no harm, while the doctor's intention may have been beneficence, to do the patient good (Beauchamp & Childress 2009).

End-of-life decision-making presents many challenges to health professionals. How can it be ensured that the patient and family's perspective is at the heart of ethical decision making? When is it appropriate to discontinue treatment and move to palliative care? How do we ensure that the benefits of healthcare interventions outweigh the harms? How can we ensure that all patients are treated fairly and that no-one is discriminated against on the basis of age, class, gender, ethnicity or any other consideration? And importantly, how can we ensure that the people in our care live well until they die?

As this book was going to press, a charter for those who are terminally ill was launched by the Royal College of General Practitioners and the Royal College of Nursing (Paige 2011). The charter will offer patients the opportunity to express their preferences and wishes in writing so that health professionals will be better able to respond to them. Such a charter is respectful of patient autonomy and has the potential to stimulate conversations regarding end-of-life care between patients and professionals. The scenario relating to Gemma relates to decision making involving parents and a seriously ill child. The ethical issues that arise relate, however, to all patient groups. It is not possible to discuss all of these issues in detail but readers are advised to access the Ethical Framework for End of Life (McCarthy et al. 2010) care to consider, in more detail, issues relating to breaking pain management, life-prolonging treatments and confidentiality.

Legal issues

The welfare principle underpins the decisions to be made in this scenario. According to s.1(1) of the *Children's Act 1989*, the child's interest must be the paramount consideration. This means all decisions must be made in the best interests of the child. However, what is in Gemma's best interest may not be clear and such decisions may be complicated by a conflict between what is in the best interests of the client, the family and the physician (O'Brien et al. 2010). This problem, which is not uncommon, is discussed in some detail in Chapter 4.

The scenario also raises legal issues about the nature of consent. The doctor may have judged that Gemma was too unwell to convey her own views but that he had respected parental autonomy, as defined by O'Brien et al. (2010), by ensuring that the person with parental responsibility for Gemma has consented to treatment on her behalf. However, the nurse may have been concerned that Gemma's voice has not been heard and that Gemma's mother felt so distressed and vulnerable at that time she could not speak for herself.

The provision of food and fluids is widely regarded as a fundamental and symbolic aspect of care, the absence of which might be interpreted as neglect and a failure in the duty of care (Ersek 2003). The nurse, however, may have seen artificial feeding as a medical treatment that was likely to impose a degree of suffering on Gemma that outweighed any potential benefits.

More generally, a health professional caring for a patient who is terminally ill and/or in receipt of futile treatment which merely prolongs life, may well be concerned that the death of the patient may be investigated to ensure that treatment has been lawful. While it is very rare for a health professional to face a charge of murder, the line between lawful and unlawful treatment is a fine one. The withdrawal of treatment or the use of drugs to control symptoms may in some cases accelerate death. Decision making in such circumstances is difficult but the judges have been of some help in this complex area. The following cases provide some guidance for the health professional, in the context of symptom control.

R v Bodkin Adams [1957] Crim LR 365

The Doctor had benefitted from the wills of a number of elderly patients. The circumstances were suspicious and he was charged with the murder of an 81 year old patient, who had left him substantial sums in her will. In the course of summing up the case to the jury, Devlin J explained that 'murder was an act or series of acts ... which were intended to kill, and did in fact kill.' He went on to say

> If the first purpose of medicine, the restoration of health, can no longer be achieved, there is still much for the doctor to do, and he is entitled to do all that is proper and necessary to relieve pain and suffering even if the measures he takes might incidentally shorten life by hours or perhaps even longer.

Dr Bodkin Adams was acquitted.

R v Arthur (*The Times* 6 November 1981)

Dr Arthur, a paediatrician, was caring for a baby with Down's Syndrome. He wrote the child up for nursing care only and also prescribed a powerful pain killer not usually given to babies. The child died. Dr Arthur was charged with attempted murder. The jury accepted that the Doctor had not intended to kill the baby but to enable the child to die peacefully. Dr Arthur was acquitted.

The decision may be more difficult if it means that treatment is withdrawn. It must be remembered that a patient who has capacity may always refuse to undergo or to continue treatment of any description regardless of the consequences of that decision. This was made clear in the following case.

B (adult refusal of medical treatment sub nom Ms B v NHS Hospital Trust [2002] EWHC 429

Ms B, aged 43, was paralysed from the neck down. Her life was maintained by ventilation. Ms B withdrew consent to the ventilation whereupon those caring for her decided that she lacked capacity and that the treatment should be continued. When the case came before the court it was decided that Ms B had capacity. Dame Elizabeth Butler-Sloss stated the position very clearly when she said

> ... a seriously disabled person has the same rights as the fit person to respect for personal autonomy. There is a serious danger ... of a benevolent paternalism which does not embrace recognition of the personal autonomy of the seriously disabled patient.

Ms B's refusal of treatment must be respected.

In 1993 the House of Lords (now the Supreme Court) was faced with the issue of whether or not treatment could be withdrawn. The decision has proved to be very important as the judges took an overview of all the relevant law in this context. The case is usually simply referred to as '*Bland.*' Details are given below.

Airedale NHS Trust v Bland [1993] 1 All ER 821 (House of Lords)

Anthony Bland was one of the victims of the Hillsborough disaster. As a result of his injuries, he was left in a persistent vegetative state (PVS) with no prospect of recovery or improvement. His family and the health professionals caring for him asked the Court for a declaration permitting withdrawal of life sustaining treatment, including artificial hydration and nutrition, to allow the patient to die peacefully suffering the least pain and distress. The declaration was granted. In the course of his judgment, Lord Goff said:

> I am of the opinion that there, when such treatment has no ... no absolute obligation upon the doctor ... to prolong his life, regardless of the circumstances. ... I cannot see that medical treatment is appropriate or requisite simply to prolong a patient's life , when such treatment has no therapeutic purpose of any kind, as where it is futile because the patient is unconscious and there is no prospect of any improvement in his condition.

All five judges agreed that treatment could be withdrawn.

One of the important points made in *Bland* was that such issues should be debated in Parliament and that the law should be changed if that were deemed to be appropriate. So far Parliament has declined to act.

We have, however, seen some change in the context of assisting suicide. By the *Suicide Act 1961* s.2(1) it is a criminal offence to 'aid, abet, counsel or procure the suicide of another'. The availability of physician assisted death in other countries, especially in Switzerland, has led to some degree of compromise. While relatives or friends who facilitate a person's journey to such clinics can be said to be in breach of the *Suicide Act*, the Director of Public Prosecutions has issued guidance indicating how any decision whether or not to prosecute in such cases will be made. (Available at www.cps.gov.uk)

It is now perhaps unlikely that a person who facilitates a physician assisted death will face prosecution. The law has not been changed, the *Suicide Act* being described by the European Court of Human Rights as 'designed to safeguard life by protecting the weak and vulnerable.' (*Pretty v UK (2002) 35 EHRR 1*).

The debate about whether or not the law governing end-of-life decisions is satisfactory continues. Do take the opportunity to discuss these issues with other health professionals.

Professional issues

Differences in professional values may have played a key role in the differing perspectives of the nurse and doctor in this scenario. Austin et al. (2009) identify how doctors are often primarily focused on cure and treatment but nurses' chief concern is more likely to be holistic care and comfort. Similarly Robertson (1996) identified that nurses will often give priority to patient autonomy and promoting patient choice in circumstances where physicians tend to regard beneficence as of greater significance. It is also important to take into account differing degrees of power and authority and the extent to which it is culturally acceptable for doctors to be challenged by other health professionals (Schulter et al. 2008).

The nurse might have regarded Gemma as having such a poor quality of life that prolonging it further through advanced treatments was not warranted. Quality of life, however, is a subjective concept, bound up with individual beliefs and attitudes and it is important not to assume an appreciation of the quality of someone else's life. Whiity-Rogers *et al.* (2008) stress the importance of emotional engagement with the experiences of patients and their families to gain an understanding which will be critical in helping them make decisions. Family centred care is, indeed, at the heart of children's nursing and nurses have a key role in advocating for the patient and family in end-of-life care decisions (Thacker 2008).The NMC (2008) and HPC (2008) equally argue that professional–client relationship based on openness trust are the hallmark of professional practice.

It is also evident that without good inter-professional team working it would not have been possible to reach an agreed plan of care for Gemma in which her interests were protected.

Conclusion

The scenarios presented within this chapter illustrate the extent to which people who are in need of healthcare often face fundamental transitions in their lives and may be highly vulnerable. It is a privilege for health professionals to be in a position to make such a difference to clients' experiences at these times. However, it is also essential that the trust placed in them is justified by the maintenance of quality care which is supported by application of relevant legal, ethical and professional principles.

It is not always easy to fulfil the expectations made of health professionals who may face significant obstacles to the delivery of an aspired standard of practice. These difficulties may be linked to individual competence and capability but might equally be located within a hostile environment. If health professionals find themselves constrained from carrying out practice in accordance with their judgements they may experience significant anguish. It is important to recognise such 'moral distress' which can lead to a poorer quality of care, decreased job satisfaction and staff turnover as well as people choosing to leave the health professions.

Attention has been drawn to the significance of 'ethical climate' in the reduction and management of moral distress. A good ethical climate can allow health professionals to overcome the challenges they encounter and enable positive core values, centred upon clients' wellbeing, to be enacted in everyday practice. A positive ethical climate is characterised by a number of features such as open channels of communication and collaborative working. Other relevant factors which have been identified include access to adequate resources, managerial support and ongoing education.

Thus, the promotion of professional healthcare practice requires an understanding of the complexities underpinning care and is the responsibility not just of individuals but the teams and organisations in which they work. It is argued that health professionals, working with a strong commitment to professional values and equipped with relevant knowledge and skills, are well placed to drive such practice development.

References

Austin, W., Bergum, V. & Goldberg, L. (2003) Unable to answer the call of our patients :mental health nurses experience of moral distress. *Nursing Inquiry,* 10(3), 177–183.

Austin, W., Kelecevic, J., Goble, E. & Mekechuck, J. (2009) An overview of moral distress and the paediatric intensive care team. *Nursing Ethics,* 16(1), 57–68.

Beauchamp, T.L. & Childress, J.F. (2009) *Principles of Biomedical Ethics (*6th ed.). Oxford University Press, Oxford.

Corley, M.C. (2002) Nurse moral distress: a proposed theory and research agenda. *Nursing Ethics,* 9(6), 636–650.

Corley, M.C., Minick, P., Elswick, R.K. & Jacobs, M. (2005) Nurse moral distress and ethical work environment. *Nursing Ethics*, 12(4), 381–390.

Dlugacz, Yosef (2010) *Value-Based Health Care Linking Finance and Quality.* Wiley, USA.

Elpern, E.H. (2005) Moral distress of staff nurses in a medical intensive unit. *American Journal of Critical Care,* 14(6), 523–530.

Erlen, J.A., (2001) Moral distress: a pervasive problem. *Orthopaedic Nursing,* 20(2), 76–80.

Ersek, M.(2003) Artificial nutrition and hydration. *Journal of Hospice and Palliative Nursing,* 5(4), 221–230.

Griffith, R. (2008) Protecting children key principles. *British Journal of Midwifery* 16(12), 322–323.

Griffith, R. & Tengnah, C. (2010) *Law and Professional Issues in Nursing* (2nd ed.). Learning Matters, Great Britain.

Gutierrez, K.M. (2005) Critical care nurses' perceptions of and responses to moral distress. *Critical Care Nursing,* 24, 229–241.

Hamric, A.B. (2000) Moral distress in every day ethics. *Nursing Outlook,* 48, 199–201.

Health Professions Council (2008) *Standards of Conduct, Performance and Ethics.* HPC, London.

Holly, C. (1993) The ethical quandaries of acute care nursing practice. *Journal of Professional Nursing,* 9(2), 110–115.

Jacobs, H.H. (2005) Ethics in pediatric end-of-life care: a nursing perspective. *Journal of Pediatric Nurisng,* 20(5), 360–369.

Jameton, A. (1984) *Nursing Practice::The Ethical issues.* Englewood Cliffs, Prentice Hall. New Jersey.

Jameton, A., (1993) Dilemmas of moral distress: moral responsibility and nursing practice. *Clinical Issues in Perinatal Women's Health Nursing,* 4(4), 542–551.

Kalvemark, S., Hoglund, A.T., Hansson, M.G., Westerholm, P. & Arnetz, B. (2003) Living with conflicts-ethical dilemma and moral distress on the healthcare system. *Social Science and Medicine,* 58, 1075–1084.

158 Jane Leng and Deborah Macartney

Kelly, B. (1998) Preserving moral integrity: a follow up study with new graduates. *Journal of Advanced Nursing,* 28(5), 1135–1145.

Lutzen, K., Blom, T., Ewalds-Kvist, B. & Winch, S. (2010) Moral stress, moral climate and moral sensitivity among psychiatric professionals. *Nursing Ethics,* 17(2), 213–224.

McCarthy, J., Donnelly, M., Dooley, D., Campbell, L. & Smith, D. (2010) *Ethical Framework for End-of-Life Care.* The Irish Hospice Foundation, Dublin (See http://www.hospicefriendlyhospitals.net/ethics Accessed 1 June2011).

Mohammed, S. & Peter, E. (2009) Rituals, death and the moral practice of medical futility. *Nursing Ethics,* 16(3), 292–302.

Nathaniel, A.K. (2002) Moral distress among nurses. *The American Nurses Association Ethics and Human Rights Issues, Updates* 1(3).

National Patient Safety Agency (2009) *Being Open: Communicating Patient Safety Incidents with Patients, Their Families and Carers,* UK.

Nursing and Midwifery Council (NMC) (2008) *The Code: Standards of Conduct, Performance and Ethics.* NMC, London.

O'Brien, I., Duffy, A. & O'Shea, E. (2010) Medical futility in children's nursing: making end of life decisions. *British Journal of Nursing,* 19(6), 352–356.

Olson, L.L. (1995) Hospital Ethical Climate Survey, available: Linda L. Olson, PhD, RN, CNAA olson@sxu.edu.

Olson, L. (1995) Ethical climate in health care organisations. *International Nursing Review,* 42(3).

Paige, J. (2011) Royal Colleges create charter for terminally ill patients, *The Guardian* 01/06/2011 (http://www.guardian.co.uk/society/2011/jun/01/charter-for-terminally-ill-patients Accessed 1 June2011).

Pauly, B., Varcoe, C., Storch, J. & Newton, L. (2009) Registered nurses' perceptions of moral distress and ethical climate. *Nursing Ethics,* 16(5), Canada.

Pijl-Zieber, E., Hagen, B., Armstrong-Esther, C., Hall, B., Akins, L. & Stingl, M. (2008) Moral distress: an emerging problem for nurses in long term care? *Quality in Ageing,* 9(2), 39–48.

Reason, J. (2008) *The Human Contribution: Unsafe Acts, Accidents and Heroic Recoveries.*

Redman, B.K. & Fry, S.T. (2000) Nurses' ethical conflicts: what is really known about them? *Nursing Ethics,* 7, 360–366.

Robertson, D. (1996) Ethical theory, ethnography and differences between doctors and nurses in approaches to patient care. *Journal of Medical Ethics,* 22, 292–299.

Schulter, J., Winch, S., Holzhauser, K. & Henderson, A. (2008) Nurses' moral sensitivity and hospital ethical climate: a literature review. *Nursing Ethics,* 15(3), 304–321.

Silva, D.S., Gibson, J.L., Sibbald, R., Connolly, E. & Singer, P.A. (2008) Clinical ethicists perspectives on organisational ethics in healthcare organisations. *Journal of Medical Ethics,* 34, 320–323.

Stark, Z., Hynson, J. & Forrester, M. (2008) Discussing withholding and withdrawing of life –sustaining medical treatment in paediatric inpatients: audit of current practice. *Journal of Paediatric Child Health,* 44(7–8), 399–403.

Sundin-Huard, D. & Fahy, K. (1999) Moral distress, advocacy and burnout: theorising the relationships. *International Journal of Nursing Practice,* 5, 8–13.

Thacker, K.S. (2008) Nurses' advocacy behaviours in end of life nursing care. *Nursing Ethics,* 15(2), 174–184.

Thompson, C. & Dowding D. (2002) *Clinical Decision Making and Judgements in Nursing,* Churchill Livingston, London.

Wilkinson, J.M. (1987/8) Moral distress in nursing practice: experience and effect. *Nursing Forum,* 23(1), 16–29.

Zuzelo, P.R. (2007) Exploring the moral distress of registered nurses. *Nursing Ethics,* 14(3), 344–359.

We hope you have enjoyed your journey through the book. You should have begun to appreciate that ethical, legal and professional issues are inter-related and that an understanding of all three areas is necessary for you to practise as an accountable professional. The chapter authors and editors have aimed to produce a book that will help you to apply learning to practice situations. It is likely that you will have concluded that, although there are differences in terms of the roles and scope of practice of different health professionals, there is much common ground. All health professionals must, for example, understand the meaning and implications of consent (Chapters 3 & 4), truthtelling (Chapter 5), confidentiality (Chapter 6) and justice (Chapter 7) for their practice.

It is hoped that in your everyday practice you will work with colleagues who demonstrate a high level of professionalism and who prioritise patients' well-being and interests. Working well as part of a multi-professional team requires that there is mutual respect and trust. It requires also that there is a forum for professionals to get together and discuss issues relating to patient care. It is important to remember that all health professionals can make an important contribution to the patient experience. When standards of professional practice are lowered due to individual, organisational or political failings, patient dignity and safety is compromised. When there are high standards of professional practice, the dignity and safety of patients is prioritised. Health professionals can feel proud and privileged to contribute meaningfully and positively to the experience of patients and families.

In preparing this text, we aimed to help you to increase your understanding of the fundamental principles relevant to practice. The ethical, legal and professional principles and guidelines examined underpin your actions and omissions. Turning a blind eye or omitting to act when unprofessional practice is witnessed, is not an option. Being a health professional requires engagement and commitment to professional practice and does not support the role of detached bystander.

We hope that working through Chapters 8 and 9, and the other chapters in this text, will strengthen your sense of professionalism in practice and provide you with resources to respond effectively should you witness unprofessional practice.

You have chosen to practise in a very exciting, rewarding and ever-changing field. Changes resulting from research, policy, political initiatives, demographic trends and patterns of illness and disability impact on your professional practice. You need to keep up-to-date with such changes and approach them critically asking: How do these changes impact on the patient experience? And how do such changes impact on the ethical, legal and professional aspects of my practice?

We recommend that you continue to engage with developments in empirical research, and philosophical scholarship, in ethics. This can help you to understand, for example, how individual professional practice can be facilitated by the ethical climate of healthcare organisations. It can also help you to be more critical as you engage in discussion where an understanding of key concepts may be assumed and, perhaps, misunderstood. Concepts such as dignity, quality (of life), sanctity (of life), futility, consent, autonomy and confidentiality need to be interrogated before meaningful discussion regarding how they relate to the patient experience can proceed. You can have an important role here in raising questions and sharing your understanding with colleagues. You are also likely to benefit from understanding theoretical developments in healthcare ethics, for example, in ethics of care.

In relation to the law, changes occur as injustices are acknowledged and remedied. However Parliament has a habit of identifying a problem and then passing an Act to deal with it. The fundamental principles generally do not change although detail will certainly do so. One example of this is found in the *Mental Capacity Act 2005*, dealing with perceived problems of ensuring that the most vulnerable in society have their interests fully and properly considered when decisions are taken about them or their treatment (see Chapter 4). The end-of-life issues discussed in Chapter 9 continue to be of importance as society's views in relation to physician assisted death evolve. You may remember that the present law relating to suicide is found in the *Suicide Act 1961*. This Act marked a very great change as, until that time, to attempt to commit suicide was punishable as a criminal offence. A more humane approach is now taken which respects an individual's autonomous right to commit suicide while at the same time protecting those who are vulnerable from undue influence or coercion.

Developments in relation to the regulators of the health professions continue and again, it is important that you keep abreast of these. Checking the websites of the NMC and HPC will keep you informed of changes to the professional codes and also to changes in the Fitness to Practice processes and regulation more generally. We recommend that you do this regularly.

We wish you well as you develop your professional practice and careers. An interesting time lies ahead.

Further reading and resources

Further Reading

Banks, S. and Gallagher, A. (2009) *Ethics in Professional Life: Virtues for Health and Social Care.* Palgrave Macmillan, Basingstoke.

Brykczynska, G.M. and Simons, J. (2011) *Ethical and Philosophical Aspects of Nursing Children and Young People* (1st ed.). Wiley-Blackwell, Chichester.

Chadwick, R., ten Have, H. and Meslin, E.M. (Eds) (2011) *The Sage Handbook of Health Care Ethics: Core and Emerging Issues Sage.* Los Publications Ltd, London.

Clements, L. and Thompson, P. (2007) *Community Care and the Law* (4th ed.). LAG.

Cribb, A. (2005) *Health and the Good Society: Setting Healthcare Ethics in Social Context.* Oxford University Press, USA.

Dimond, B.C. (2011) *Legal Aspects of Nursing* (6th ed.). Pearson Education, London.

Fennell, P. (2011) *Mental Health Law and Practice* (2nd ed.). Jordans Publishing, Bristol.

Herring, J. (2009) *Family Law* (4th ed.). Pearson Education, Harlow.

Jecker, N.S., Jonsen, A.R. and Pearlman, R.A. (2007) *Bioethics: An Introduction to the History, Methods, and Practice.* Jones and Bartlett Publishers, Sudbury.

Letts, P. (Ed.) (2010) *Assessment of Mental Capacity – A Practical Guide for Doctors and Lawyers* (3rd ed.). British Medical Association and the Law Society, London.

Loewy, E.H. and Springer Loewy, R. (2010) *Textbook of Healthcare Ethics* (2nd ed.). Springer, New York.

Mason, J.K. and Laurie, G.T. (2011) *Mason and McCall Smith's Law and Medical Ethics* (8th ed.). Oxford University Press, Oxford.

Matiti, M.R. and Baillie, L. (Eds) (2011) *Dignity in Healthcare: A Practical Approach for Nurses and Midwives.* Radcliffe Publishing, London.

McCarthy, J., Donnelly, M., Dooley, D., Campbell, L. and Smith, D. (2010) *Ethical Framework for End-of-Life Care.* The Irish Hospice Foundation, Dublin – http://www. hospicefriendlyhospitals.net/ethics

McHale, J. and Fox, M. (2007) *Health Care Law – Text and Materials* (2nd ed.). Sweet & Maxwell, London.

Murray, S.J. and Holmes, D. (2009) *Critical Interventions in the Ethics of Healthcare.* Ashgate, Farnham, Surrey.

Stanford Encyclopaedia of Philosophy – http://plato.stanford.edu/

Ten Have, H.A. and Hans-Martin, S. (2010) *Consensus Formation in Healthcare Ethics.* Springer, New York.

Journals

Bioethics – http://www.wiley.com/bw/journal.asp?ref=0269–9702

Cambridge Quarterly of Healthcare Ethics – http://journals.cambridge.org/action/displayJournal?jid=CQH

Ethics and Social Welfare – http://www.tandf.co.uk/journals/resw

Journal of Family Law – http://www.Jordanpublishing.co.uk/online-services/family

Journal of Medical Ethics – http://jme.bmj.com/

Journal of the Legal Action Group – http://www.lag.org.uk/legalaction

New Law Journal – http://www.newlawjournal.co.uk/nlj

Nursing Ethics – http://nej.sagepub.com/

Online Journal of Health Ethics – http://www.ojhe.org/

The Hastings Center Report – http://www.thehastingscenter.org/Publications/HCR/Default.aspx

Web-sites

British and Irish Legal Information Institute – http://www.bailli.org

Department of Health – http://www.dh.gov.uk/en/home

The Ethox Centre – http://www.ethox.ox.ac.uk/

General Medical Council – http://www.gmc-uk.org/

The Hastings Center – http://www.thehastingscenter.org/

Health Professions Council – http://www.hpc-uk.org/

The International Centre for Nursing Ethics – http://www.surrey.ac.uk/fhms/research/centres/icne/

Nursing and Midwifery Council – http://www.nmc-uk.org/

Official Website of the European Union – http://www.europa.eu

UK Clinical Ethics Network – http://www.ethics-network.org.uk/

World Health Organisations – Ethics and Health – http://www.who.int/ethics/en/ – Law – www.who.int

Acts of Parliament can be accessed at http://www.legislation.gov.uk

Department for Education – http://www.education.gov.uk

Justice – http://www.gov.uk/guidance/protecting-the-vulnerable

http://www.gov.uk/law.commission/index.htm

Index